The Spark In The Street

The joy of ministering to the homeless and the poor - the "least of these."

Jean-Luc

ISBN: 1497444616
ISBN 13: 9781497444614

Library of Congress Control Number: 2014908537
Createspace Independent Publishing Platform
North Charleston, South Carolina

Contents

CHAPTER one

You Were Born For A Purpose

Part 1

God Will Use You

Y ou have yet greater things to do for the Lord God in your life than ever before. God has a plan on how to do that. I am not speaking as such to established pastors and leadership in denominational and independent churches. I am speaking to YOU, on Main Street; you of humble heart. Hardly anyone knows you. Yet, you are the ones God IS going to use powerfully when Jesus said, in **John 14:12:**

"I tell you the truth, anyone who has faith in me will do what I have been doing. He will do even greater things than these, because I am going to the Father."

God has a plan on how to use you powerfully. You were born for a purpose; you will do great things! God knows you, and he knows exactly where you are. He loves you and cares for you and He will use YOU mightily! You, the quiet ones, the ones waiting in the wings; prepare to be called to duty in the service of the Lord. The world will stand amazed at the mighty works of the Holy Spirit through you, as you joyfully and lovingly minister to the "least of these" - the homeless, the poor, those in need.

"But God chose the foolish things of the world to shame the wise; God chose the weak things of the world to shame the strong. He chose the lowly things of this world and the despised things – and the things that are not – to nullify the things that are..." (I Corinthians 1:27)

Also:

"Blessed are the meek, for they will inherit the earth." (Matthew 5:5.)

Please note that the Lord did not say, the "weak", but the "meek;" the humble.

You, saints of God, have felt the Lord Jesus Christ tugging at your heart concerning serving Him and about revival in the land. Every saved person has a calling on their life to exercise their God-given gifts to glorify God. Many of you know the gifts of the spirit which are in you and you are longing to have them manifested in your life and used for God's glory. The Lord has put a longing deep within your soul to preach or teach, prophesy, heal the sick, feed the poor, write, do miracles and wonders, be a missionary, become a pastor, sing or play a new music, evangelize, organize home meetings, or be an intercessor, etc. Some of you haven't told anyone of these powerful inner feelings. However, God knows...He put them there!

For one reason or another you have found it difficult, if not impossible, to start your ministry in your life or release your gifts and calling. If you go to church, you may quietly occupy a pew or seat and the church may hardly know you're there.

You might even have come to a point where you wondered if these inner thoughts of being used of the Lord were your own thoughts rather than God's will for your life.

PLEASE, DO NOT GIVE UP OR DOUBT ANY LONGER IF IT REALLY WAS THE LORD SPEAKING TO YOUR HEART!

Some of you have heard His quiet voice within you for years. Know that the Lord's gifts (everyone has them) and calling are irrevocable **(Romans 11:29)**. He HAS gifted you and He WILL use YOU. Everyone who submits to Christ's purpose in them will be used mightily of the Lord. The Lord will release those gifts in you so that your longing to serve Christ Jesus will be fulfilled. He is Lord of your life and He is Lord of your gifts. Your gifts are God's grace manifested through you.

"But to each one of us grace has been given as Christ apportioned it. This is why it says: 'When he ascended on high, he... gave gifts to men.'" (Ephesians 4:7, 8)

Theologians, educated religious leaders, pastors, evangelists and revivalist who think highly of themselves have complicated the subject of revival and how to be used of the Lord. The Lord, however, has made it so simple, a child can be used powerfully of the Lord. Jesus loves to use the simple (you and me!) to confound the wise.

"...I praise you, Father, Lord of heaven and earth, because you have hidden these things from the wise and learned, and revealed them to little children. Yes, Father, for this was your good pleasure." (Luke 10:21)

The participants of this service to the Lord have no age limit. The very young to the very old can and will be used by the Lord. A Bible College degree is not a prerequisite (in fact, it could even be a hindrance). The Lord, through the Holy Spirit, will be your teacher. This which the Lord will do in and through you has biblical and spiritual integrity. It will not be chaotic or confusing. Every word, work, miracle, healing – every one of your actions and words – will point to Jesus Christ as Lord of all for the salvation of souls. God will joyfully receive all the glory which you were created to joyfully give Him.

"Let us rejoice and be glad and give him glory!" (Revelation 19:7)

Part 2

What Is In Your Heart?

In the subsequent chapters, you will learn how to start, develop and take your ministry to the front lines in the street. "In the street" means outside of the confines of the church walls. You will find out what to do and what not to do, what to say and what not to say, what to bring and what not to bring, what to give and what not to give. All this will be shown to you according to God's plan. You will read clear and detailed information on how to minister to "the least of these;" the homeless, the poor.

You may have a desire to skip the introductory chapters and go directly to those chapters that give you the distilled information you seek. However, please do not skip these introductory chapters which will prepare you for this powerful ministry. What is in your heart is just as important as what is in your hand to give to the needy. These chapters are to prepare your heart to do mighty things and give glory to God. You are not alone, as God does have a plan.

Saints of God, you must check your heart to see what is in it. If you have a problem seeing your true heart, ask the Lord to reveal it to you - have him search your heart. You must ask the Lord as the psalmist asked in **Psalm 139:23-24:**

"Search me, O God, and know my heart; test me and know my anxious thoughts. See if there is any offensive way in me, and lead me in the way everlasting."

At one point in this ministry I had to ask myself about "violence." Being in the street could be dangerous, I reasoned. What if I was attacked? Would I defend myself with violence, in the same way that I would be attacked? Could I react violently to physical provocation? There was a particular incident, at one point, that could have turned bad.

A brother and I were bringing some bean burritos to a camp where I ministered once a week. There usually were anywhere from four to eight homeless men (and sometimes women) in this camp near the heart of town. When I got there, there seemed to be about twenty people who were suddenly rushing me to reach for the limited available food. To further complicate the issue, the camp I normally fed was white and the people rushing me were black! If I had said, "No," to the black homeless people and fed only the whites, I could have insulted some people and maybe started a fight, as the black group was somewhat drunk and belligerent.

The white group was rather young and passive. However, the black homeless men were not waiting any longer and reached in my bag themselves (I usually pass the food out myself) and they started pushing me to get to the food. I had to sternly tell them to get their hand out of the bag. I felt like slapping their hands and yelling at them to back off, as they reached in my bag! For a split second, I thought about bringing a baseball bat with me next time I came here! Just for a split second. Appropriately, the white homeless men sternly admonished them not to reach into the bag, and to wait their turn. The black group was so forceful, they received all the bean burritos initially meant for the expectant (white) group (as they waited for me every week, always at the same place and time.)

When they all saw that there was no more food left for me to give away, everyone walked away to eat at their spot on the grass, under the trees or on a bench. However, four men in the white group did not get food, as there was not enough left. We had not planned on feeding this many people. At this point, I could have become angry at this out-of-control situation. I am basically a non-violent person. However, once in a while I did have dreams at night about beating up the bad guys! A definite and final decision had to be made about non-violence.

I checked my heart. What was there? Lord, I prayed for you to fill by heart with your love.

I felt compassion for the blacks who were so hungry. I did not see this as feeding hungry, aggressive men. I saw this as feeding Jesus. I do not feed the homeless or the poor...I feed Jesus. You understand? I felt bad for the whites for whom the food was meant in the first place, but who did not get fed. For the sake of peace, they did not take any food. Only one white man got a bean burrito, and he split it in half with someone else. I felt love for both the white and the black camp.

I then went to the remaining whites who had not eaten and praised them for their patience and humbleness. I told them that if they could wait just a little while, I would go get them some food. My brother in the Lord and I then went to the closest hamburger place and bought each of them a big, delicious hamburger. When we got back, I didn't get out of my truck but waved them over and discreetly gave them their food while blessing them in the name of Jesus. I say "discreetly" because we did not want to be rushed again by a mob which was still there. We found out later that a false rumor had been spread that free fried chicken would be given out at this place and time. No wonder there were so many hungry people waiting to be fed.

There must be order and good management on your part. There cannot be any violence or hate or even any thought of it – none of it in your heart whatsoever. In this age of grace, violence does not give God glory. There can only be compassion and love even when you are taken by surprise. Settle that in your heart before you start this ministry. You cannot yell at them, grab them or call them names! You can't even frown at the "least of these!" No violence! Not even in your thoughts. Trust God – He will watch over you.

"And the Lord's servant must not quarrel; instead, he must be kind to everyone, able to teach, not resentful. Those who oppose him he must gently instruct, in the hope that God will grant them repentance leading them to a knowledge of the truth, and that they will come to their senses and escape from the trap of the devil, who has taken them captive to do his will." (2 Timothy 2:24-26)

Understand that we are all a work in progress and settling these issues in your heart and soul may take more than one day. However, do it quickly with earnest prayers to God, remaining sensitive to the guidance and teaching of the Holy Spirit.

"Everyone should be quick to listen, slow to speak and slow to become angry, for man's anger does not bring about the righteous life that God desires." (James 1:19-20)

"The good man brings good things out of the good stored up in his heart...For out of the overflow of his heart his mouth speaks." (Luke 6:45)

During this incidence, I should have kept my eyes on Jesus rather than the storm. I should have rebuked evil rather than rebuking men. At this point, I decided in my heart that I would never show violence to anyone and at any time. Neither would I raise my voice. If I was to be attacked while in the performance of my ministry, they would have to do to me as they wanted. I was feeding Jesus and Jesus would protect me. I trust my Lord. If it's my time to die, then so be it. I carry my cross with me every day. The more I do God's will in my life, the more likely the enemy will want to nail me to the cross! Glory to God!

You seriously have to ask yourself what is the desire of your heart. You must know for a fact and accept deep down in your soul that the desire of your heart must first be to please your Lord and Savior Jesus Christ by your faith and to glorify His Holy Name by your actions.

"Delight yourself in the Lord and he will give you the desires of your heart." (Psalm 37:4)

CHAPTER *two*

Jesus Is The One Who Sends, Trains,

Ordains And Anoints You

Part 1

To The Least Of These

A young man wanted to be a pastor. He would speak of it continually but was not financially or otherwise able to attend Bible College. He lamented (expressed sorrow) because he thought he would never be able to be a pastor. The church he attended would not use him in that capacity nor were they able to train him. Still, in his heart he knew God wanted him to be a pastor. It was his heart's desire. But how?

One day I finally told him he could be a pastor. He asked me how that could be possible. I told him about a bridge in our town under which camped some homeless people I knew and to whom I had ministered. I took him under the bridge, introduced him to the homeless guys there and said to him, "Behold, your flock." And to the homeless I said, "Behold, your pastor!" I then told him to feed his sheep, minister to them and take good care of them. Though I mentored him, Jesus was about to train him for the desire He had put in that young man's heart. The homeless received him and were glad to have him as their "pastor!"

If you have a shepherd's (a pastor's) heart, go and pastor. If you have a yearning to preach, go, as there are thousands of millions who need to hear you. You want to teach, do it now. You can. Just teach what you know and have learned by faith. Are there some now who are not getting healed because you are not praying for them? Do not wait. Go and pray for the sick. God will meet you there, where your heart meets His. Are there some who are being overcome with evil? Go and intercede for them in the quiet of your prayer closet.

You do not have to go to Africa or Asia or some other faraway place as a foreign missionary to be used of the Lord. Just go in the street! That is, go outside the church walls. Go first in your neighborhood, your city, your school, your immediate environment. There are so many close to your home who are in such great need.

You say you cannot get your pastor or church leadership to "send" you? Saints of God, listen to me - Jesus is the one who sends you, trains you, ordains and anoints you. Stay in touch with The Master! As wonderful as your pastor may be, it is not him who gives you spiritual gifts and sends you out. Jesus graces you with gifts, anoints you and sends you out; and your pastor may acknowledge that fact.

It's funny how we want the church establishment to recognize us. Yet, God is the first and only one from whom we should seek to be called. We are not here to please man, but to please God. I have nothing against the church except when it holds back the saints of God from using their God-given gifts, and so preventing them from serving the Lord Jesus Christ more fully and bringing glory to His Name. There are many people, not just in the rest of the world, but in your very own neighborhood or workplace who are in darkness and who need to be saved, healed, comforted, fed and clothed, set free, encouraged...

"The harvest is plentiful, but the workers are few. Ask the Lord of the harvest, therefore, to send out workers into his harvest field. Go!" (Luke 10:2-3)

A few saints of God are sent by the Lord to minister to the wealthy, to kings, leaders of countries and to the powerful and well-known. However, there are only a limited number of these to whom one can minister and there are so many saints who want to minister but don't know where to start. There are so many more poor people in this world to minister to than to the few wealthy. The Lord may send you to the wealthy and powerful, but this book is about the rest of the hungry people in the world who are begging for you to come and minister to them. They are most often called "the least of these."

You may not be a spark in the high echelons (ranks) of Hollywood or Washington, D.C. Nevertheless, you can be a spark in the streets of your neighborhood or city. This could very well start a great spiritual fire and deeply impact more people's eternity than ministering in Washington, D.C., or Hollywood.

"Consider what a great forest is set on fire by a small spark." (James 3:5)

Who are "the least of these?" The expression appears in **Matthew 25:40:**

"...whatever you did for one of the least of these brothers of mine, you did for me."

"Brothers of mine" has been defined by some bible scholars as just the apostles, or maybe only the Jews, or it could be those who will be saved and belong to Jesus. It is a crucial verse because it shows that what you do for the least of these, you do it for Jesus. When you feed the poor, you feed Jesus. So, who are the "least of these?"

After you have been ministering in the street for a while, you may start to wonder what you are doing there. The devil may try to make you lose your focus by telling you the "least of these" are not important. That's when you respond that you are not doing it to the "least of these," but to Jesus Christ!

"For I was hungry and you gave me something to eat, I was thirsty and you gave me something to drink, I was a stranger and you invited me in, I needed clothes and you clothed me, I was sick and you looked after me, I was in prison and you came to visit me." (Matthew 25:35, 36)

The righteous answered, "When did we do all that to you, Lord?" That's when Jesus answered, "Whatever you did for one of the least of these...you did for me." We have the beginning of a list of who the least of these are; the hungry, the thirsty, the strangers, the naked, the sick, those in prison. Who are the "least of these? There are more.

Part 2

Your Rewards, Blessings, Protection And Healing

"He who is kind to the poor lends to the Lord, and he will reward him for what he has done." (Proverbs 19:17)

There is a reward for being kind to the poor and taking care of the "least of these!"

"...blessed is he who is kind to the needy." (Proverbs 14:21)

"Blessed is he who has regard for the weak; the Lord delivers him in times of trouble. The lord will protect him and preserve his life; He will bless him in the land and not surrender him to the desire of his foes. The lord will sustain him on his sickbed and restore him from his bed of illness." (Psalms 41:1-3)

These are such loaded verses! If you regard the weak (the least of these), this is what the Lord promises:

1. You are blessed
2. You will be delivered in times of trouble
3. You will be protected
4. Your life will be preserved
5. You will be blessed in the land
6. You will not be surrendered to your foes (enemies)
7. You will be sustained on your sick bed
8. You will be restored to health

Wow! What a great blessing there is to be had for taking care of the needy, the weak, the "least of these." Not only will the Lord protect you, but there is also healing in it for YOU! You want your healing, help the weak. Who are the "least of these?"

"If there is a poor man among your brothers...give generously to him and do so without a grudging heart; then because of this the Lord your God will bless you in all your work and in everything you put your hand to. There will always be poor people in the land. Therefore I command you to be open handed toward your brothers and toward the poor and needy in your land." (Deuteronomy 15:7, 10, 11)

Can you handle more blessings for taking care of the poor, the "least of these?"

9. You will be blessed in your work
10. You will be blessed in all you put your hand to

Give freely to the poor and the needy and the Lord will bless you at your job or business! Giving to the poor is a command. However, give out of the love which is in your heart for "the least of these." Let your heart be pure in this matter.

"If anyone has material possessions and sees his brother in need but has no pity on him, how can the love of God be in him? Dear children, let us not love with words or tongue but with actions and in truth." (1 John 3:17, 18)

Certainly, there is a reward in this world for your ministry to the poor. However, your true reward is when you see Jesus face to face on that day and He says to you, "Come, you good and faithful servant."

Do you know who the "least of these" are?

"Has not God chosen those who are poor in the eyes of the world to be rich in faith and to inherit the kingdom he promised those who love him?" (James 2:5)

Many of the poor are rich in faith; they love Jesus their Savior with all their heart; and they will inherit the kingdom. We are witness to this here in the street. The homeless depend from day to day, hour to hour completely on Jesus for their daily subsistence (needs). They are often very close to starvation, cold, heat, disease, theft, injury and assault. They know that without faith in Jesus, they simply would not survive. I would venture to say that I have found at least 90% of homeless (and poor people) to be saved or be very receptive to the Word of God for salvation! We are located in the Southeast United States, but you may find different results in other parts of America or wherever you may find yourself in the world. The least of these will amaze you with their strong faith in Jesus Christ. THEY will minister to YOU about faith!

So, what should you do? As James so well said, "Faith by itself, if it is not accompanied by action, is dead." You must get out of your home and get out in the street. You must get out of the church and get in the street. You want to get closer to Jesus, get in the street. You want to grow in Christ and in His amazing love, get in the street. You want to see healing, signs and wonders, get out in the street. In the "street" means outside of the church walls.

This book will show you how to get started and how to grow in your ministry. Whatever you do, go!

"All authority in heaven and on earth has been given to me. Therefore go..." (Matthew 28:18)

I understand that some of you may be homebound and getting out in the street may not be feasible. There are ministries for all who want to serve the Lord. The biggest need, of course, is the need for INTERCESSORS. You could also have a ministry on the Internet or on the phone. I know someone who writes LETTERS to servicemen overseas to encourage them and to let them know someone is praying for them. In our town, we have a ninety-two year old woman who makes homemade quilts and gives them away to the homeless in the wintertime! I will address these and other ministries you can consider further in subsequent chapters.

CHAPTER three

Be Like Jesus!

Part 1

You Are Called Of The Lord

In this book, I will give you the real world application of the written Word in the Bible concerning your calling. If you wonder if you are called or not, rest assured...YOU ARE called of the Lord to serve Him and to glorify His Holy Name. Since you are reading this book, consider yourself called! If you have read the Bible and are saved, consider yourself called of the Lord Jesus Christ to serve Him in some capacity, according to the gifts He has given you. If you want to serve him quietly and meekly, so be it. If you have it in your heart to serve him with power, with signs and miracles, so be it. He wants to use YOU! He already has put in your heart how he wants to use you. Not only does God want to use you, but He searches the whole earth to find people through whom He can work.

"For the eyes of the Lord run to and fro throughout the whole earth, to show himself strong in the behalf of them whose heart is perfect toward him." (II Chronicles 16:9 KJV)

"Perfect" in the above scripture means completely, fully, wholly. So, if you are completely, fully, wholly given to God's purpose in you, He WILL find you because He IS looking. You might say, "But I'm not trained for the ministry," or, "I'm not able." That does not matter. God does not call the "qualified;" He qualifies the called! If it is in your heart to serve God, He will find you and He will train you. What is in your heart? What is your heart's desire?

"God looks down from heaven on the sons of men, to see if there are any who understand, and who seek God." (Psalm 53:2)

Believe me, saints of God, you may understand much more about the Word of God than many pastors, preachers and evangelists I have known! You may have been through the pains of learning faith, as taught by the Lord. There are many leaders in the church who have never been at the front lines of spiritual warfare. You may be able to preach the Word, not because you have a Bible College degree, but because you have learned the Word by faith, in the street. You were so close to the enemy that you have seen the whites of his eyes! And you came out victorious, covered by the blood of Jesus. You called on the name of Jesus and He found you, and you have not been the same since.

You have been told that you cannot serve the Lord because you were soul deep in drugs. Maybe, you stole, or sold, or injured or killed...and you went to prison. Maybe you have simply been married more than once and so are forever banned by the leaders of the church for service to our Lord who, by the way, is looking for you to serve Him and glorify His Holy Name! Maybe you lied, cheated or who knows what other sin drew you away from the love of Jesus Christ. But the blood of Jesus shed on the cross for you broke away all shackles and chains that bound you to that past life. You are now free in Christ Jesus to live the life He has for you, empowered by the Holy Spirit which He has given you.

Paul, the writer of half of the New Testament was giving instruction to Timothy on how to serve when he said:

"Even though I was once a blasphemer and a persecutor and a violent man, I was shown mercy... But for that reason I was shown mercy so that in me, the worst of sinners, Christ Jesus might display his unlimited patience as an example for those who would believe..." (1 Timothy 1: 13, 16)

Do not let your past or even your present faults prevent you from serving the Lord in a powerful ministry. You are NOT the sum of all your past mistakes. Your sins were nailed to the cross with Jesus. Guilt is one of the biggest tools of the devil. He tells you that you are not worth serving the Lord, and you just can't do it. He tells you even God doesn't want you to serve Him. Just stay home. Don't go in the street. Don't go outside the church walls. Stay safe in the church and maybe people won't ask too many questions about you and your past, and embarrass you.

Nowhere in the Bible does Jesus ever say to anyone, "Stay safe!"

You tell that devil that you are forgiven by the blood of Jesus on the cross for past sins, present sins and future sins. When the devil reminds you of your past, you remind him of his future! The Lord loves you. There is nothing you can DO to make Him love you. He already loves you and died for you. THERE IS NOTHING YOU EVER NEED TO DO TO MAKE HIM LOVE YOU. God has always loved you unconditionally and always will. In fact, **"God IS love!" (1 John 4:16).**

You have been to the front lines. You have been where most people have not gone. You are ready for the calling of the Lord to lead captives (prisoners) out of the enemy's camp. You have no qualms about riding in the enemy's camp at full speed, slaying the enemy and taking back what the enemy has stolen from you. You now seek the Lord, your Commander in Chief, that He may use you more fully. If you seek Him, He will find you and use you mightily. You will glorify the Lord our God!

Nobody may know how you truly feel in your heart about being a warrior for God. But God knows! You have shared your heart about this subject with very few people because you feared that most would just laugh at you (especially your family). However, there is a time coming very soon, saints of God, when the Lord will call His mighty army who is quietly waiting in the wings and YOU will boldly answer. The church leadership and those that scoffed at your heart's desire to serve the Master will stand in amazement that your prayers are being answered, as the sick are healed, the blind see, the deaf hear and the poor are fed and blessed!

"...Christ suffered for you, leaving you an example, that you should follow in his steps." (1 Peter 2:21)

Part 2

You Are Like Jesus

"Your attitude should be the same as that of Christ Jesus." (Philippians 2:5)

It is not presumptuous (meaning overconfident or arrogant) to want to be like Jesus. Jesus WANTS you to be like Him! Most people will laugh at you if you say, "I want to do what Jesus did." If those that scoff at you are Catholics, they may say, "Do you think you are a Saint?'"

Actually, saints are those who are saved and are faithful and devoted to God **(Psalms 4:3, 31:23).** The Hebrew word for saints (or godly) appears twenty-six times in Psalms alone. In New Testament sense, YOU are a saint of the God of Israel if you are saved!

To some that would say, "Do you think you are perfect," you would answer, "No, but I am being continually perfected." Thought God will meet you wherever you are, He will not let you stay there long. He will teach you to be like His Son.

**"Be perfect, therefore, as your heavenly Father is perfect."
(Matthew 5:48)**

Your present physical being may not be perfect, but that Holy Thing which is in you is perfect and does things through you which are perfect. God has put in you His divine nature so that you could be like His Son.

1. You have His DIVINE NATURE.

**"He has given us his very great and precious promises, so that through them you may participate in the divine nature..."
(2 Peter 1:4)**

Also, from the very beginning of creation, God made you to be life Himself.

2. You are created in THE IMAGE OF GOD.

"So God created man in his own image, in the image of God he created him;" (Genesis 1:27)

What does it mean to be made in the image of God? It means God gave you His attributes. You, also, want to love and be loved. You want others to be saved and be in the family of God. You want to create. You do that not only through having children, but also in art and science. You create music, dancing, paintings, sculptures, etc. Humans create new plants and genetic engineer animals to serve our purpose. You have that nature of God in you which wants to create. You have a mind that searches for God, as He gently and lovingly calls for you, his sons and daughters.

**"For we are God's workmanship, created in Christ Jesus to do good works, which God prepared in advance for us to do."
(Ephesians 2:10)**

3. You have THE MIND OF CHRIST.

"We have the mind of Christ." (1 Corinthians 2:16)

"Everything that I learned from my Father I have made known to you." (John 15:15)

You may say, "I sure don't feel like I have the mind of Christ. I do such stupid things sometimes." Is the Bible false, then? Let me tell you - YOU HAVE THE MIND OF CHRIST! Believe the Word of God. Jesus has given you His Holy Spirit to dwell in you and to teach you all things you need to know to serve the Lord in word and in power. As He teaches you over a period of time, you come to realize more and more the immense, wonderful presence of that Holy Thing which is within you; the mind of God. If you did not have the mind of God, you would not be able to be saved.

4. You have received THE HOLY SPIRIT

"We have not received the spirit of the world but the Spirit who is from God, that we may understand what God has freely given us. This is what we speak, not in words taught us by human wisdom but in words taught by the Spirit, expressing spiritual truths in spiritual words."
(1 Corinthians 2:12, 13)

You are one with God. When I say "you are" or "you have," please understand that there is a process by which you learn these spiritual precepts. It is like saying to you before the fact, "You are a doctor." It may take you twelve years of education after high school to realize it. It is in you, but it took twelve years to realize it and eventually to do the things that doctors do and bring healing to a hurting population.

However, as the end is at hand, know that the Lord will speed things up. As we say in my neck of the woods, "It ain't gonna be as long as it has been!" So, buckle up, saints of God, and keep your eyes on Jesus!

"For the Lord will carry out his sentence on earth with speed and finality." (Romans 9:28)

"I am the Lord; in its time I will do this swiftly." (Isaiah 60:22)

So far we can see that you are not only made in the image of God, but you also have the mind of Jesus, the nature of God, and the glory that God gave Jesus. You see, you are not only a physical being but also a spiritual being. You are one with Jesus and the Father.

5. You have THE GLORY OF GOD.
6. You have JESUS IN YOU.

"...Father, just as you are in me and I am in you. May they also be in us so that the world may believe that you have sent me. I have given them the glory that you gave me, that they may be one as we are one: I in them and you in me." (John 17:21-23)

The word "glory" here is the Greek word *doxa* which means; awesome light and splendor that radiates from God's presence and is associated with his acts of power and speaking of words of excellence. That is in you! Because God's glory has been given to you, you are able to show it to the world. That is accomplished by you loving others, ministering to the "least of these," bringing souls to salvation and in Holy Spirit signs, miracles and wonders.

More and more, others will see in you a reflection of Jesus as you grow in the love of Jesus Christ. There are places, such as public schools, your place of work and, increasingly, our military forces, where you may not be able to openly mention the name of Jesus Christ. However, as you minister with the love of Jesus (without even mentioning the name of Jesus), people will come to YOU and tell you, "You're a Christian, aren't you?" They will know because they will see the "glory" of God which is IN you, and manifested (shown, evident, obvious) THROUGH you.

"Live such good lives among the pagans that...they may see your good deeds and glorify God..." (1 Peter 2:12)

If that was not enough:

7. You are THE SALT OF THE WORLD.
   You can give the world that Holy flavor!

"You are the salt of the world." (Matthew 5:13)

8. You are THE LIGHT OF THE WORLD.

"You are the light of the world...So, let your light shine before men, that they may see your good deeds and praise your Father in heaven." (Matthew 5:14, 16)

Do you still have a problem accepting who you are in Christ and all the benefits that come with being an adopted son or daughter of the Most High God? I haven't even mentioned, yet, that Satan was defeated at the resurrection of Jesus and that monkey is off your back. What is holding you back from serving the Lord with mighty Holy Spirit power? Nothing! Is it easy? No! Can you do it? Yes! You are more than conquerors. Yes, you CAN do all things in Christ Jesus. Nothing is impossible with God!

Take Paul, for example, that amazing, most educated disciple of Jesus who contended in the name of Jesus with the greatest minds of his time and preached the word with signs and wonders following. This is the man who also wrote half of the New Testament. It was not as easy for him as you may think. He was still in a man.

"I do not understand what I do. For what I want to do I do not do, but what I hate I do." (Romans 7:15)

Yes, you will still goof up, from time to time. You will have urges you wished you didn't have. You will say or feel things you shouldn't. You will fall. And you will pick yourself back up and keep on going. You will continue to allow the Holy Spirit to keep on perfecting you.

Don't listen to the "naysayer" and **"Aim for perfection" (2 Corinthians 13:11),** and seek to be like Jesus. Believe me, you wanting to be like Jesus flatters His Father! What father would not want to bless the one who not only says good things about his child, but wants to be like him?

Jesus wants you to be like Him and do the things He did.

"Anyone who has faith in me will do what I have been doing. He will do even greater things than these, because I am going to the father." (John 14:12)

9. Jesus is IN YOU.

I know that it is hard to fathom how you can do greater things than Jesus did. Jesus tells you this because He sent the Holy Spirit to dwell in you. That is, Jesus is IN you. God is IN you. So, let Him work in and through you. Jesus said in **John 17:11;**

"Holy Father, protect them by the power of your name – the name you gave me – so that they may be one as we are one."

"I have made you known to them, and will continue to make you known in order that the love you have for me may be in them and that I myself may be in them." (v. 26)

10. You are also SENT BY JESUS.

"As you sent me into the world, I have sent them into the world." (John 17:18)

Jesus tells us, as He was sent by His Father; we are sent also. The things He did, we are to do, also...and greater things! You don't want to be like Paul. You don't want to be like Abraham, or Moses, or Gideon, though they were great men of God and are great examples to us. You want to be like Jesus! Jesus dying on the cross and sending you the indwelling of the Holy Spirit makes that possible. Don't let ignorant men talk you out of that. Now, don't back up; don't be ashamed, and complete the work God gave you to do. Go, be like Jesus and glorify the Father as Jesus glorified Him when He said in **John 17:4;**

"I have brought you glory on earth by completing the work you gave me to do."

CHAPTER *four*

The Invisibles

Part 1

Your Mind On The Street

If you want to find out something about the homeless, you should ask the homeless. Not all will be candid with you. However, if you find one that is willing to speak to you, buy him a meal and fellowship with him.

One mid-morning, I invited such a man to eat with me at a breakfast restaurant in my neighborhood. He took about twenty minutes to order while he was talking about the origin of his homelessness, and how he was really not poor but wealthy because of land he owned "up north." After about twenty minutes of indecision, he finally ordered a bowl of chili with crackers...lots and lots of crackers.

We talked at length about how one becomes homeless and how his whole family hated him. While speaking he would make ketchup cracker sandwiches...one cracker on the bottom, a big squirt of ketchup, and one cracker on top! At one point, he casually said, pointing at a man with a bicycle passing by, "You see that man there? He's homeless."

I didn't know that.

More ketchup cracker sandwiches. More discussions on the psychosis present in a few of the homeless. A few minutes later, he turned again towards the big picture window next to our table facing the main highway and said, "You see that man there walking with a backpack? He's homeless."

Really?

The waitress delivered his bowl of chili which he immediately topped with a mountain of crumbled crackers...while still eating ketchup cracker sandwiches on the side. He shared how he really was a street preacher, and he didn't really have to be there if he didn't want to, except the Lord had given him that ministry. He is a servant of the Lord. Then he suddenly stopped, looked at me and declared, "I don't think I've eaten in a restaurant in six years." He then raised his eyes to heaven and announced, "God, I love this food!"

I said, "The bowl of chili?"

He paused and looked at me, "No, man, these ketchup crackers. God, I love them!"

He could have ordered anything. I thought that he, as a homeless person, would have been hungry. He could have had twenty-seven eggs over-easy, one garden shovel full of hash-brown potatoes and all the bacon from three large pigs! This was his big chance.

As he popped one more ketchup sandwich in his mouth, washing it down with orange juice, he said, "You see these two guys across the street, they're both homeless." He didn't even raise his head to look, it seemed. I didn't even see him look outside the big picture window. After he had pointed out homeless people about six times in fifteen or twenty minutes, I finally said, "You're putting me on. All these guys cannot be homeless. There can't be that many homeless people in my neighborhood!"

"Oh... there are many more than that," he replied casually between bites of chili, crackers, ketchup cracker sandwiches and gulps of orange juice.

I was doubtful that I was getting the truth from this fellow. He was a rather odd individual! After all, this is MY neighborhood. "How do you know that?" I questioned.

He stopped eating and looked up at me momentarily with a blank stare, not believing that I didn't truly believe him, "I slept with them last night...I mean, we all slept in the same place...that patch of woods three blocks down," as he quickly pointed with one hand while the other hand was making another ketchup cracker sandwich. Then he proceeded to tell me all their names and individual personality traits. "You see that one there, the young one, he won't talk to anyone...don't talk at all. You can give him food, though; he'll take it. Give him the food, bless him in the name of Jesus and go. Leave him alone. He won't talk. Must be something wrong with him. He always sits at the bus-stop...every day...but never takes the bus."

He told me the street where the bus stop was located. I'll have to look.

Then he added, matter-of-fact, "Did I tell you my father stole my girlfriend from me, and now they're living together? Man, my family really hates me!"

Had he planned it right, he could have left the restaurant with enough food to last him for a whole week. As it is, when we left he asked for and got just a handful of crackers, which seemed to have made him very happy.

The next day, as I rounded the corner where the named bus-stop was located, I looked and sure enough I saw the young, bearded homeless man sitting there motionless with a blank stare. On later occasions, I have stopped to give him food. He would take it but never speak. I would always bless him in the name of Jesus, telling him Jesus loved him. And I would leave. One day as I drove away, I looked back at him, with his blank stare, silently eating his hamburger I had just given him. Though I did personally bless him in the name of Jesus, I would, from time to time, also pray for him when he was on my heart.

Then one day he stopped coming to the bus stop. I never saw him again after that. Sometimes, our window of opportunity for ministering to the "least of these" opens and closes rather quickly.

The key lesson in all this was that, "I looked in my neighborhood with the homeless in mind, and I saw them." I had never seen him before, yet he had been right there at the bus stop every day as I drove by. Why had I not seen him? I needed to keep my focus on "the least of these" in the street.

Part 2

Your Eyes On The Street

All the homeless men that were pointed out to me were not only in my neighborhood, but on the road that I traveled every day. Yet, I had not seen them. The day after I ate brunch with my unique homeless guest I took that road again and paid attention. I made it a point to seek and see. However, I had not driven a hundred yards before I found my mind wandering to other subjects...and the sights around me disappeared! It happened that quickly. How did that happen?

I'm sure you do the same thing. If you have riders in your car, it is almost impossible to pay attention to the homeless people around you unless they are holding a large cardboard sign to let you know. You may casually glance at them but never register that this is someone to whom you can minister the love of Christ Jesus.

If you are alone in your vehicle, you may listen to the news or be immersed in listening to your music. You may be thinking about the chores you have to do today or what you must do at the destination to which you are driving. You may be balancing your checkbook or deciding what to cook for dinner tonight. You may have a "million" thoughts going through your mind. You may even be praying or worshiping as you are driving.

However, if you don't see that homeless person on the side of the road and stop to minister to him right there and then, he may end up going hungry that day or sleeping in the cold that night without a warm coat or blanket you could have given him. It is very well possible you could be the only one that day to stop and offer a comforting word to let him know he is loved. You may stop and be the only one that week to pray for his needs and let him know that Jesus loves him...and that if Jesus loves him, you love him too. And if you shake his hand, you may be the only person by whom he was touched in the past month. The human touch is so important and so painfully missed.

Gentle words are important. Shared prayers are important. Faith is important. But faith without works is dead. So always leave something physical with them...a hamburger, a cold/hot drink, a coat or shirt, a pair of socks, shoes, a blanket, a couple of dollars...

"Suppose a brother or sister is without clothes and daily food. If one of you says to him, 'Go, I wish you well; keep warm and well fed,' but does nothing about his physical needs, what good is it? In the same way, faith by itself, if it is not accompanied by action, is dead." (James 2:15-17)

(We will discuss in future chapters the numerous needed and acceptable things that you can leave with a homeless person)

You must train yourself to "see" the homeless. That will take work because to the world they are invisible. You may be too busy with the cares of life to notice those that are suffering, those you are able to help. Sometimes, you may see a homeless person and truly not be able to stop. Make a note of that spot and plan on stopping sometime on your way back. Most homeless people have their own "territory" they return to daily.

When you are looking for the homeless, you are really looking for Jesus. When you give the homeless a drink, you are giving Jesus a drink. When you give them a coat, you are giving Jesus a coat. When you love the homeless, you love Jesus Christ.

"...whatever you did for one of the least of these brothers of mine, you did for me." (Matthew 25: 40)

I tell you the truth, many of the homeless in our region (Southeast United States) are saved, born again, baptized, going-to-heaven Christians. Yes, Jesus calls them "brothers of mine." The majority of the homeless are brothers of Jesus! They are His family. They are God's children. If Jesus was on the side of the road, would you see HIM? Now, if you can't see the homeless, maybe you are not seeking Jesus. If you do not stop to love them, maybe it's not important for you to take time to stop and tell Jesus that you love Him.

Sometimes, it's an effort to stop on a busy day and acknowledge Jesus Christ as the one you love. One way you can do that is to stop and give much needed, healing love to a homeless person, thus "doing it" to Jesus. When your world stops so that you may love on one of God's precious children, how blessed you will be! You cannot out-give God. He is a rewarder of those who diligently seek Him.

No matter how you may get distracted while driving, eating in a restaurant, or walking about, work hard at seeing those precious homeless children of God...and take a moment to bless them. You may notice them because they are wearing a backpack. You might catch them out of the corner of your eye because they are riding a bicycle in no special hurry. Their ill-fitting, stained clothing may betray them. Most often, with no definite destination, they appear to have a blank look on their faces as they wander around aimlessly. They may be drunk. Stop and minister to them. The drunk will be blessed if you give him something to eat...and he will be eternally grateful (he will remind Jesus about what you did when he gets to heaven!). You've done it to Jesus, and Jesus is watching.

You may say, "Let them get a job. Why should I work so some drunk can eat?"

Please understand, they are homeless because they have one or more personal issues. There is one thing you can say about all homeless people – they all have issues! That's why they're living in the street. In other words, they are handicapped in one way or another. Some have serious issues, but you be at peace. Looking at their issues could be like looking at the storm and being scared. Rather, look at the God of the storm, and trust Him and bring peace to the "least of these."

You might say, "They can walk. They are able bodied, so they can work." Saints of God, their handicap may not be physical. In fact, most of their handicaps are emotional and/or mental. An emotional handicap can be as debilitating (weakening) as a paraplegic who must use a wheelchair.

Why judge them? They are not the only ones with issues. You have them, also! "An issue" could be described as a problem deep in your heart which you keep repeating and have difficulty solving on your own. These issues may be drug or alcohol dependency, involvement in pornography, greed, a bad temper, poor self-esteem, abuse as a child, poor family relations (ineffective parents), etc. These issues result in bad decisions and hinder greater success in your life.

Your issues may not be so severe that you cannot function in a fast-paced society. However, I suspect many people could be borderline street people and may be susceptible to being easily pushed into homelessness. We all have issues. The homeless issues are obviously more serious and handicap them.

If you knew a handicapped person in a wheelchair with no use of his legs, would you tell him, "Get out of that chair and get a job. I'm not helping you!" God forbid! Homeless people are similarly handicapped. Yet, we drop what we are doing in order to compassionately give assistance to someone in a wheelchair, but we are blind to the homeless who could sometimes be considered more severely handicapped.

There are some who say, "Since they are Christians, they should be able to get out of the street and get a job. Let them show their trust in the Lord." Would you tell that to the wheelchair bound paraplegic? "You are a Christian, so get out of your chair and walk. What's wrong with you, don't you trust the Lord? How come you can't walk yet? Why are you still in that wheelchair?"

Saints of God, once you understand the homeless peoples' handicap, you will start to see them throughout your day just as easily as you see someone in a wheelchair. You will momentarily drop what you are doing to compassionately minister to their needs in the love of Christ Jesus.

"Religion that God our Father accepts as pure and faultless is this: to look after orphans and widows in their distress and to keep oneself from being polluted by the world." (James 1:27)

Part 3

Your Heart On The Street

Pick a day of the week and go feed some of the homeless. Pick up a load of bean burritos or hamburgers and drive down a street, perhaps downtown, or where the homeless may congregate. Stop by a homeless person and say, "Are you hungry? Can you use a warm, fresh Taco Bell bean burrito?" (Please, do not brashly ask, "Are you homeless?")

Of course, this gives you the opportunity to minister the love of Jesus to them. Take one or two brothers (or sisters) with you who you may be training for this ministry. Have them bring bottled water and something sweet. Drive until you see a homeless person and then pull over to stop and ask him if he is hungry.

(I use the masculine form of a noun or pronoun throughout my writing, but it could very well be feminine also; him/her, brother/sister. I am not being sexist! I use the masculine form exclusively in this whole book for simplicity's sake only)

As you drive down the street, focus on "seeing" the homeless – recognizing who is homeless and in need of a hot bean burrito (they stay warm for a long time). Certainly, you may know many of the homeless in your town and where their personal areas are. However, the homeless population is always on the move and constantly changing. So, you want to look for new homeless people you have never ministered to before. That means you have to pay attention to the road while driving and look for signs of homelessness in the people you are seeing.

The problem is that, often, the people riding with you in your vehicle want to talk about everything except the homeless. They want to talk about what they think at the moment; what they've done the past week; what so-and-so said at church; uncle Bob's ingrown toenail surgery; whether they like garlic or not; how old grandma is getting to be; the terrible boss they have; how they like wearing white socks; what they do with stale bread; the latest political drama out of Washington...blah, blah, blah! Unable to focus, you drive right by many homeless saints of God. It is frustrating, as it does not fulfill God's will for that precious moment.

Before hitting the road, you may have said a prayer asking God for direction; that you may find the homeless He wants you to minister to, and for His Holy Spirit blessing in and through you. Please take note; after that point, only the homeless should be on your mind, heart and lips. You need to focus on the task at hand. You are not there for your own self but for the sake of the homeless. Quit talking about yourself and mind how you are going to find and minister to the homeless!

Stay sensitive to the direction and will of God while you "seek to see" the homeless. Stay in an attitude of prayer, praise and worship. You are taking the church out into the street. Be respectful of Holy Spirit presence and guidance, as you would if you were IN the church (building).

Sometimes you will notice a number of homeless people together near one place. You may not be able to minister to all of them at once. The Holy Spirit will speak to your heart as to which one you need to feed, with whom you can share your testimony of Jesus Christ or who needs prayer. You need to rest in the Lord and be in an attitude of prayer while driving or walking the road in order to see as Jesus sees.

As you minister to the homeless, do not talk about yourself at all. Lavish ALL your attention on the ones to whom you are ministering. You are not in a position of ministry to glorify yourself. Ask for their names, but do not give your name unless they ask. The name you want them to see when they look at you is the name of Jesus.

For example, after you've handed Tom food and drink:

"What's your name?"

"My name is Tom."

Shake hands or pat on the shoulder, "Good to know you, Tom. God bless you, brother. Jesus loves you, forgives you and He heals you. Is there anything we can pray to Jesus for you?"

After they get to know you, you will be getting hugs, rather than handshakes! They will also ask you to pray for them.

Tom didn't ask for your name, and you didn't volunteer it.

They don't want to know about your job, your car, your house or what you do. Why would you tell them about yourself; to make them envy you, to show how much more you have or know? How shallow and self-serving. They will know you and respect you when you are consistent in your love for them.

When you go minister to the "least of these," don't wear your best clothes. Dress down. Do not wear your jewelry, best shoes, or even your watch. No shirt and tie, and especially no suit - ever! If you hit the street after church, change first. Bring your iPhone in case someone who doesn't have one needs to make a call home, or other important call.

Instead of the glory of your life, what should they see? Yes, that's right; they should see the glory of Jesus. You are the way that Jesus shows love to the poor and homeless. You are to be a reflection of Jesus. Remember, you are a work in progress, so be patient with yourself and with the Lord.

When you are motivated by the love of Jesus Christ in your heart, you are most likely to do the right thing. God knows which homeless person needs His love and who needs healing. Only

God knows the heart of man and He will guide you to the right homeless person if you stay sensitive to the heart of God.

You are taking the church out of the church walls and into the street. During that time, quit idle, self-centered chatter, and stay in an attitude of prayer as you would in your own church. Give thanks to God that you may glorify His Holy Name, as He guides you in the ministry to which He has called you.

Ministering to the homeless is a tender, gentle, loving and sensitive ministry to rough, hurting, cold and hungry men and women whom God loves so very much as His own precious children. It is a time for you to forget the world, give fully of yourself and "carry your cross."

If the previous sentence slightly irks you and you feel a tinge of reluctance, you may need to diligently search the Word of God and your heart. You may need to spend more time on your knees with your face to the ground in serious, humble prayer to the Lord.

However, if you truly resent that same sentence about "carrying your cross," you may just want to find something else to read that is more entertaining than his book. Or just give this book to someone who is not offended but rejoices in the expression "carry your cross." If you are not willing to "carry your daily cross," you will be missing out on the greatest task to which a human being can be appointed; ministering the love of Jesus Christ to a hurting and hungry world.

For the rest of you saints of God who look expectantly for the promises of the Word of God to be manifested in your lives, I challenge you to experience a personal revival as you grow in ministering to the "least of these." You will be led by the Holy Spirit to discover the path which will lead to true Holy Spirit revival, not only in yourself, but also in your neighborhood and throughout your city. I guarantee you that God has the perfect plan to accomplish this in you. The time is at hand; you can be, and will be, a spark in the street.

"If anyone would come after me, he must deny himself and take up his cross daily and follow me." (Luke 9:23)

"...and anyone who does not carry his cross and follow me cannot be my disciple." (Luke 14:27)

CHAPTER *five*

Entertaining Strangers

Part 1

All Of Heaven Is On Your Side

Years ago, I pulled into the parking lot of a strip mall where the sandwich shop was still open late in the evening. As I approached the Subway Store, I saw the shadow of a man sitting on a plain, flat concrete bench about ten feet in front of the entrance door. All the other stores were closed except the sandwich store and another store a couple of doors down on the right. The man on the bench came clearer into focus as I walked closer.

His sat with drooping shoulders, wearing clothes that seemed to be as old as he was – maybe just over sixty or so. His stained polo shirt seemed to have been handed down many a time before it got to him. His jeans were probably older than his polo shirt. However, his face was more weathered than either the polo shirt or the jeans!

As I walked closer, I saw a tanned, dirt-caked face riddled with the wrinkles of a long, harsh homeless life. His uneven, matted grayish hair was topped by a torn and faded ball cap. The shadow of his beady eyes sunken into their sockets betrayed his malnutrition. He did not seem to have the strength to look up at me or speak to me as I walked by and stepped into the sandwich shop. He had no backpack or bag at all. He clearly was one of the invisibles!

I ordered my Subway sandwich and drink and looked out the picture window where I could still see the back and drooping shoulders of the old homeless man on the bench. The more I thought about him, the more compassion welled up within me. I turned to the young sandwich maker and asked him to make me another sandwich just like the one I had ordered for myself. I was going home to eat, and on the way to my vehicle I would let the old homeless man have a sandwich. As my sandwiches were being made, I pondered this man's situation and silently prayed for him. When my order was completed, I walked outside.

As I stood in front of him to ask him if he was hungry, he lifted his unshaven face to look at me and the dark shadow hiding his eyes disappeared. He grinned, and I saw his watery eyes open wider. I handed him the sub sandwich, and his grin turned to a smile. I told him to go ahead and open it up to make sure it's what he could eat. He glanced at it and quietly and slowly unwrapped it. Before eating it, he looked up at me and raised his bruised and scratched hand to shake mine.

As I stood there watching him, I could smell the body odor of a man who hadn't bathed in probably a month. Every crease in his unwashed hand had brown dirt in them and his long, curved, smoke-stained fingernails all hid some kind of black stain. The back of his hand had a couple of small, healing open sores.

I was repulsed for a moment! I was thinking of words like "health risk," "sanitation," "diseases." However, I also thought that this man may not have touched or been touched by anyone in months. How good it would be for him to shake someone's hand – to feel the warm touch of another human being.

Again, compassion and love flooded my soul for the least, the lost and the last. How can I tell him about the love of Jesus if I am not able to show him love? I grasped his hand firmly in mine. It's all right; I can always wash later on! We didn't shake; we just held clasped hands for a moment, as his whole face lit up in a life giving smile. Then, he let go of my hand, grabbed the sandwich with both hands and took a big bite. Now, I was smiling. Through all this, he never spoke a word or uttered a sound.

I walked away to go to my vehicle with my sandwich and drink in hand. I then realized that I didn't need this drink - I can drink at home. How could I leave him without a drink? I had taken only five steps when I turned around to go back and give him my drink. I looked at the bench and just froze there with a bagged sandwich in one hand and a drink in the other.

He was gone!

He was just taking a bite of a sandwich before I took five hurried steps and turned around. I looked to the right and to the left. Nothing. How could this man move so fast? I went back in the sandwich store and asked if they had seen an old homeless man come in. Nothing. I checked their bathroom to see if he had gone in without being seen. Nothing. I went to the store two doors down and did the same thing. Nothing. There was no way this man, in his shape, could wrap the sandwich back up, pick it up and sprint to the end of the mall – or wherever – and disappear in that short period of time.

I went back later, during daylight, and sat on the same bench, pondering. I had brought a tape measure with me to see how far he had to go to disappear while I took five steps. I measured and timed it all. He would have had to do the 100 yard dash in less than ten seconds...holding a sandwich in his hands...with a mouth full...not to mention his awful physical shape! The fastest record holding sprinter on Earth can do it in maybe 9.90 seconds.

There can be only one solution to this enigma (puzzle):

"Do not forget to entertain strangers, for by so doing some people have entertained angels without knowing it." (Hebrews 13:2)

I took five steps and he disappeared. That is not natural - it is supernatural.

He never said a word, and though he took a bite of the sandwich, I did not see him swallow it (if that means anything.) For a while I felt fortunate that I had not neglected an angel of the Lord. After all, I did give him food and I was going to give him a drink. In my heart, I did feel compassion and love for him. I prayed for him. I felt pretty good about myself. However, not until much later did I realize that I really had not done enough.

Had I truly cared, I would have asked him about his health. I could have gone to the store to buy him some disinfectant wipes to clean himself, and bandages to cover the wounds on his hand. I could have asked him if he needed anything else or if there was anything else I could do for him. Could I have given him a ride somewhere? I had nail clippers in my pocket which I could have given him. I could have given him some food for the next day. Did he need warm clothing, socks, shoes, a sleeping bag, a backpack? I could have left a little money with him, if nothing else.

I didn't ask him if he was saved or even mentioned the name of Jesus.

In all reality, I hadn't done much at all. Did I go to the cross for him? Did I feel his desolation? After mentioning entertaining angels in **Hebrews 13:2, verse 3** continues;

"Remember those in prison as if you were their fellow prisoners, and those who are mistreated as if you yourselves were suffering."

Why does God send angels to test us, anyhow? God, who knows everything, knows our heart towards these things. The Lord could just come into our heart and look and see what's going on there. Then, He could just have His Holy Spirit teach us what we should do. But...

"Are not all angels ministering spirits sent to serve those who will inherit salvation?" (Hebrews 1:14)

So, Jesus sits on His throne, calls an angel, and commands that angel to leave heaven and go to earth and minister to you. Why? Because God so loves the homeless, the poor, the destitute, and the least, that he would send not only His Son to die on the cross, and the Holy Spirit to dwell in you, but also angels to minister to you.

All of heaven is on your side so that you can minister to the "least of these" the way God wants you to...with the love of God, not wanting that any should perish but have everlasting life. If so many people in the street do not know what love is, how will they understand that there is a God in heaven who loves them and wants them to spend eternity with Him? You are the one who will show them love so they may see, experience, and receive love, and maybe then understand why Jesus died for them on that horrible cross.

That's why you, yourself, carry your daily cross; so they may see an example of the sacrifice of Jesus dying on the cross for them. Then they may believe the gospel message which you give them; that they may trust in the name of Jesus Christ and be saved, and have everlasting life.

"We are therefore Christ's ambassadors, as though God were making his appeal through us." (2 Corinthians 5:20)

CHAPTER *six*

Moving Forward

Part 1

The Axle

If you look at a wheel, such as a bicycle wheel, you can see that in the center of it is a little circle that we call an axle. That is the center of the wheel which attaches all the other wheel parts together and to the bicycle. The axle has numerous smaller circles in it called ball bearings so that the outer circle, the wheel, may spin smoothly. Without the axle there is no functional wheel and so, no bicycle. Thus, the axle is the most important part of the wheel; a small circle (ball bearings) within a circle (the axle) within a larger circle (the wheel).

However, you say, "Maybe the tire is the most important part of the wheel." Yes, but the wheel could still spin on the inner tube and rim. This would decrease its efficiency, but it would spin.

What if the spokes of the wheel radiating out from the axle to the rim were mostly missing? The wheel would still spin though it would be a little wobbly and certainly much weaker. However, without an axle, the bicycle, as such, would be useless...forward movement would be impossible.

Obviously, you are not reading this book to learn about bicycles! Most of you are recognizing that there is a spiritual concept about to be explained which is comparable to a wheel axle. There is one part of the ministry to the "least of these" which is most important and without which there is no ministry. Other parts of the ministry might somewhat operate, but forward movement of the ministry would be impossible.

A solid foundation is important and would be represented by a thorough knowledge of the Bible. But a solid foundation without a structure built on it is meaningless. That is comparable to a ship built, but never put in the water. It would be like you knowing the Bible forward and backward, but never doing anything to serve the Lord.

A solid, level, square foundation is crucial, but you must keep building on it. You must use that foundation to continue building a sturdy structure. And what is the use of building a sturdy structure if it remains unused and empty? So, what IS this thing which is most important in this ministry to the "least of these" and ties all the pieces together?

That is... THE PLAN. God has a plan for the ministry to the "least of these." His plan ties in all the parts together and keeps them moving smoothly so that the forward movement of the ministry is possible, that it may reach its destination. Without a plan, a builder cannot build the foundation, the structure, the plumbing, the electrical, etc. A plan is necessary in order to build the whole house.

I did not come up with this plan. God did. He knows the future and He deems this plan necessary. This is the most important part of this book. All the other chapters (parts of the ministry) are important, but THE PLAN is most important because it ties in all the parts together.

THE PLAN is interwoven and explained in this whole book. To dedicate solely one chapter to it would not do it justice. In fact, just one chapter would insult it! As THE PLAN of God for your ministry and subsequent revival is woven into every part of this book, so it must likewise be interwoven within the fibers of your entire life.

The Lord wants this ministry to be REPRODUCIBLE (it must be able to be copied). It must be the same whether it is set up in Pensacola, Florida, Bulgaria or Zimbabwe. There must be a pattern that can be reproduced exactly the same, time after time, by anyone, no matter where they are in the world. Does that give you an idea of where the Lord is going to take this ministry? It will be reproducible in your neighborhood, your city, your state. If THE PLAN is not followed, the ministry's forward movement will be impossible.

God designed this plan. It's called PLAN "A." There is no plan "B." It's always been PLAN "A." This plan has been here since the beginning of time for these times now. God did not decide on this plan at the last minute. This plan has depth. In fact, it has so much depth (because it is eternal) we can't even understand the whole plan. All we can do is obey the Lord. To have this ministry to the "least of these," you must be able to obey the Lord Jesus Christ. It is not obedience to a man or to this book. It is obedience to the Builder, the One **"Through (whom) all things were made; without him nothing was made that has been made." (John 1:3).**

If you find the word "obedience" disdainful, I am truly sorry. Without obedience to the Lord, there is no ministry to the "least of these" as such. You may still go in the street, from time to time, to feed the homeless or provide some clothing for them, or other things they may need. Without obedience to God's plan for you, this might just be a hobby or activity for you. It may simply be a nice "outing" you may enjoy on a Sunday afternoon, feeding the homeless, like one may go out and feed the ducks at a pond on a sunny day.

If you want a solid, forward moving, powerful ministry with depth, then obedience to the God of Israel and to His plan is of essence. This plan will demand consistency on your part. If ministering to the "least of these" is something you plan on doing only around the "feel good" Holidays of Thanksgiving or Christmas, this is not God's PLAN. You won't be wrong, but you won't be right! You won't have a "ministry," either.

You can so far see from reading this book that if you have an aversion to (you try to avoid) certain expressions like "carrying your cross," "obedience," and "consistency," you may have a difficult time with this ministry (or any ministry). If you still feel "disdain" in your heart (disdain here means you strongly resent the above expressions and would rather I did not bring them up because it gives you heartburn), you may have to put this book down and take a strong dose of good antacid medication!

Part 2

Take Them All With You

When you go out to minister to the "least of these," you will experience all kinds of people who want to go with you for the day for all kinds of reasons. During the course of the day, you may tell these well-meaning people about THE PLAN and they will look at you with a blank stare. After all, you are "just" taking care of the homeless. What's the big deal?

There are some who are part of the "Inquisition" and will come with you to study what you are doing. They have been sent by the "Mother Church" to Judge you and see if you are a "True" Christian! Of course, only the "Inquisitors" and those like them are "True" Christians. They will check to see if you are a Branch of the "Mother Tree" that needs to be trimmed or pruned. Did you go to Bible College or Seminary? What Church sent you? What are your Church Credentials? Are you in good standing? And here's the big one; are you a LICENSED MINISTER? And don't mention THE PLAN to them because that will certainly raise some Spiritual eyebrows Heavenward!

Saints of God, a "license" is never, ever needed, to minister Jesus in any way to anyone. Licensing is something that is man-made. God never imposed the command, "Thou shalt get a license before ministering!" God is the one who calls, elects, ordains, trains and sends you out, as only He can. When He does, you will know it without a shadow of a doubt.

There are those who come with you because of casual curiosity. They appear to know everything and will respond to everything you say with, "I know." They will tell you that they've "been there" even though that was for just a half hour of ministry some years ago. They come with you for just one day so they can tell others, "Yea, I ministered to the homeless," and they can put that on their resume. They only went with you once, but they now can tell everybody how to do it. They don't have to read the book, they feel they can now write it. Mostly, they talk about themselves and how they know everything. They might even listen, out of curiosity, when you tell them about THE PLAN. However, they'll let you know they're not too sure about the plan "thing." It's just not for them.

Then, there are those who wait on the sideline until you have organized the ministry and have worked hard at it for a long while. You are barely starting to be recognized by a very few for your consistency, love and service to the homeless. These people have been keeping an eye on you and now come out of the woodwork to join you and work with you. They want to make sure it's working before they make some sacrifices and jump in with you. They work hard and are now with you all the time. However, before long they start to take all the credit for the success of the ministry. They want to preach when you have a service, and they want to tell everybody about it back at church, as if it was "their" ministry. You know they won't last or be around long because they never talk about THE PLAN.

Also, there are those who come for the novelty of it all. They are bored or need to do something different, something...fashionable. They need to be entertained. They come to see what's new and if it's fun and exciting. Are there miracles? Miracles are so much fun! Are the homeless being healed in the street? Anybody being slain in the spirit? Do crowds gather? So, where's the worship team, anyhow. You've got to have a killer worship team! THE

PLAN? What on earth are you talking about? We don't need a plan. We are saved by grace – we don't need to prepare. We're under grace, now. Jesus did it all for us, already.

These shallow kinds of people will not be with you long at all. Neither will they speak to you again because you are not sensational, or theatrical enough! You don't pray loudly enough or spit when you preach! You are simply...not entertaining enough.

Then there are those very few saints of God who shun the temptations of the world knowing those things are but temporary pleasures. They have a deep abiding love in their heart for those in life who have less than them; for injustice, for hunger, for lack. They are the ones to leave the ninety-nine sheep and go after the one errant (stray) sheep. Though others judge and condemn them, they nevertheless obediently stay on the path which God has set before them. They do not look for praise from man but keep their eyes on Jesus who keeps them, protects them, and blesses them. You may never hear of them because they do not seek fame, but live to glorify the Holy Name of Jesus Christ.

You will end up taking many kinds of people out with you to show them what you do, to train them how to minister to the homeless, and to tell them about THE PLAN. As far as I am concerned, please DO take EVERY ONE of the above out with you any time of the day or night that you are going out to minister. Since most people will not go with you, thank God for those that do! Spread your message and the love of Christ any way you can.

Your ministry does not begin nor does it end with "the least of these," but encompasses wherever you are, with whomever you are, anywhere in the world at any given time

"...be prepared in season and out of season; correct, rebuke and encourage – with great patience and careful instruction. For the time will come when men will not put up with sound doctrine. Instead, to suit their own desires, they will gather around them a great number of teachers to say what their

itching ears want to hear. They will turn their ears away from the truth and turn aside to myths. But you, keep your head in all situations..." (2 Timothy 4:2-5)

Saints of God, the Lord has a wonderful plan that not only ministers lovingly to the homeless and the poor, but also takes us in a specific direction. The street ministry is a movement forward. It has a purpose. We, the remnant, are led of the Lord, step by step, precept by precept, straight into The Revival that so many people speak about but do not know how to bring about. Ministering to the "least of these," according to God's plan, will spark the coming ground roots (street) revival. I say this by direction from the Holy Spirit.

The church establishment was offered The Revival by the Lord, but proudly turned it down because church leaders did not like how it was "packaged." This revival is packaged by the "least of these" - the poor, the homeless, the humble. Being a ground roots revival brought on by God means that this revival will not come out of the established church organization. This long awaited revival will be "street filtered." It will come out of the street, where it will be birthed (as was Jesus' ministry), and it will give ALL the praise, ALL the honor and ALL the glory to the Holy Name of Jesus Christ, our Lord and Savior.

CHAPTER *seven*

What Kind Of People Ought You To Be?

Part 1

Are There Others?

It would be a good idea to look at who else was called by God in such a manner in the past in order to understand why God would call you into a simple yet powerful ministry. Did God, at times in the past, also have THE PLAN for those saints of God who heeded the call to serve? I am not as concerned about man's record of ministries and revivals as much as I am concerned about what the Scriptures say about such subject. You might not get the whole truth from man's records, but the Scriptures will not lie or distort the truth.

We must agree on that fact, at this point, in order to understand the "solid foundation" on which we stand. The Scriptures (Old and New Testament) are the inherent word of God (inherent here means Truth and God cannot be separated) and are one hundred percent true. You may not understand all of the Scriptures, but they are nevertheless all true. I will testify that so far they have been proven completely true at every step of my life! I have observed the same in other people's lives, also, when God's Word was applied.

"All Scripture is God-breathed and is useful for teaching, rebuking, correcting and training in righteousness, so that

the man of God may be thoroughly equipped for every good work." (2 Timothy 3:16, 17)

When Jesus built the Universe and put Earth and us in it, He had a plan **(John 1:3)**. From Adam and Eve, to the resurrection of Christ Jesus and on to the "Rapture" and eternity, God has a plan. Everything in creation was done with the order and continuity of an amazing plan. The Scriptures are the record of a brief slice of that plan which pertains to us. According to THE PLAN, there MUST be a great end time revival, there MUST be a "rapture," Satan MUST be locked up in the lake of fire forever, and there MUST be a heavenly eternity for the saints of God. I say "MUST" because God is truth – He cannot lie.

This plan which I am writing about in this chapter is not a new plan. I did not invent it. God forbid! Neither did God come up with a new plan to accommodate the times. It is man himself who has invented countless number of plans to replace God's plan. It still remains that the same plan God had in the beginning is the same plan which will bring us to the end of time as we know it.

When I write that there is a plan for this ministry to the "least of these" which will lead us to an amazing revival, it is part of THE PLAN. Nothing new, just a continuation of the original, unchanging, perfect plan of God. We are called according to God's plan.

Who else did God call in the past in the same manner you are now being called? For who else did God have a calling to ministry, and a plan? Might their response then have been similar to yours now?

MOSES

Moses may have received the best education in Egypt, but forty years after he left (now at the ripe old age of eighty), we find him tending his father-in-law's flock on the far side of the desert at Horeb (which means desolation). He had been wanted by the law after murdering a man in Egypt and had been on the run ever since. Sometimes, Moses would take his flock miles from his home to look for pasture, and he would stay in the desert for many days at a time. Would you think this man to have a powerful ministry to the "least of these" (slaves in Egypt) and for him to be the leader of a great revival?

God had THE PLAN. All Moses had to do was follow THE PLAN. But Moses gave five excuses why he could not go in **(Exodus 3 and 4):**

1. Who am I that I should do this? (Chapter 3, v. 11)
2. Suppose they ask me about you (God), what shall I tell them? (v. 13)
3. What if they don't believe me or listen to me? (Chapter 4, v. 1)
4. I am slow of speech and tongue. (v. 10)
5. Please send someone else to do it. (v. 13)
"Then the Lord's anger burned against Moses..." (Exodus 4:14)

Please, saints of God, do not let this happen to you that the Lord's anger should burn against you because you are disobedient. God has a plan - just nod your head and go with THE PLAN! Of course, we know that eventually Moses followed THE PLAN, and sure enough, as odd as God's plan sounded, it worked! Would you have responded the way Moses did?

GIDEON

"Again the Israelites did evil in the eyes of the Lord, and for seven years he gave them into the hands of the Midianites." (Judges 6:1)

Times were hard because the enemy would invade every year and destroy the crops. Then, the angel of the Lord appeared to Gideon, and said, **"The Lord is with you, mighty warrior." (v. 12).** Gideon didn't look like a mighty warrior, as he was hiding behind a rock, threshing his little bit of wheat in a rock winepress to keep from being seen by the Midianites.

Gideon didn't know what was going on when he said, **"If the Lord is with us, why has all this happened to us? Where are all his wonders? ...the Lord has abandoned us..." (v. 13).** After the angel said that he was sending Gideon to go save Israel, Gideon whimpers, **"BUT Lord, how can I save Israel? My clan is the weakest in Manasseh, and I am the least in my family." (v. 15).** However, within a couple of days Gideon obeys and THE PLAN is put to work successfully, delivering Israel from the enemy and bringing revival to the Jews.

Would the "church" of today have picked such a man to lead a revival? God did because He knew Gideon's heart and He had THE PLAN. Even though God had called "the least" to execute this plan, THE PLAN worked! Gideon asked for a couple signs just to make sure and then went on with God's unusual plan. All he had to do was obey and simply follow THE PLAN. Would you have responded as Gideon did?

"The Lord does not look at the things man looks at. Man looks at the outward appearance, but the Lord looks at the heart." (1 Samuel 16:7)

DAVID

The prophet Samuel was sent by the Lord to Jesse to anoint one of his sons as King over Israel. But, which one? Though Jesse had many strong, intelligent sons (especially Eliab, v. 6), still Samuel did not get permission from God to anoint any of them. Are there any more sons? Jesse answered, **"There is still the youngest, but he is tending the sheep." (1 Samuel 16:11).**

Would a city or state have rallied behind someone like David, a very young shepherd boy in the field, as the one to lead a revival and become head of a country? Even though he didn't completely know God's plan, David, being the least of the brothers, obeyed.

This truly annoyed David's brother, Eliab, who may have been jealous and accused David of being conceited and wicked **(v. 28).** You may also get that treatment, as you enter this ministry and as you receive God's anointing!

But, you see, God has THE PLAN. David went on to fulfill his anointing over a period of fifteen years and become a man after God's own heart. He is also an important member of the genealogy of Jesus Christ. Who would have known it? God has THE PLAN. Would you have responded as David did?

"For I know the plans I have for you," declares the Lord, "plans to prosper you and not to harm you, plans to give you hope and a future. Then you will call upon me and come and pray to me, and I will listen to you. Your will seek me and find me when you seek me with all your heart." (Jeremiah 29:11-13)

"Before I formed you in the womb I knew you, before you were born I set you apart..." Jeremiah 1:5)

Part 2

The Little Circle

I probably don't have to say that to you, but the one single, most important activity you can do to prepare yourself for the ministry and for the revival is to READ THE WORD OF GOD, the Bible. Reading the Gospel of Jesus Christ not only reveals God, but it also reveals who you are in Christ. If you have read this far in this book, I strongly suspect you are very familiar with the Scriptures. After all, I am addressing Christians. If you have read the Bible beginning to end thirty-five times, then read it thirty-six times. And every time, the Lord will show you something new, something exciting; something you didn't know about Him and about you. Every time!

Familiarize yourself with THE PLAN. And then go and teach what you do know, what you have learned by faith. But you say, "I've done that and I still don't have a ministry." All right, let's get started. Now is the time.

The "word" the Lord has been giving me repeatedly for the saints for the past couple of years has been:

"Cleanse the temple of the Lord (you). Get your house in order." No ministry, nor any revival will be manifested through you until this has been accomplished in your life.

"Don't you know that you yourselves are God's temple and that God's spirit lives in you? If anyone destroys God's temple, God will destroy him; for God's temple is sacred, and you are that temple." (1 Corinthians 3:16)

We must start by cleansing the "temple" of the Lord.

You may ask, "How do I cleanse this temple? How do I start a growing ministry to the 'least of these' which will grow into a tremendous revival?" What is this great plan? What church do I go to? What organization do I hook up with? What people must I see? What Bible college should I go to (that question should be the least of your concerns)?

In answer to your questions, a small circle just big enough for you to step in would be drawn on the floor in front of you. Now, step in that circle. The greatest revival on earth starts right there, in that circle. It's not about anyone else or what the rest of the world is doing or thinking. It's about you in that little circle. You are the spark for Godly fire, beginning in your little part of the world and then spreading, as God wills (and He wills). You are important...so step into that little circle.

There was a voice long ago which told us about THE PLAN – a voice which is still valid today:

"A voice of one calling in the desert, 'Prepare the way for the Lord, make straight paths for him. Every valley shall be filled in, every mountain and hill made low. The crooked roads shall become straight, the rough ways smooth. And all mankind will see God's salvation.'" (Luke 3:4-6)

Jesus elaborated on your personal preparations in the above scripture and in the following one in order to be actively used in His kingdom. Preparations were made when He came to Earth two thousand years ago, and personal preparations are being made again for His returning.

"The time has come, the kingdom of God is near. Repent and believe the good news!" (Mark 1:15)

"Repenting" is a loaded word. Whole books can be written about repentance. You can repent for the unscriptural errors of your church. You can repent for the ungodly direction your city is taking. You can repent for the wayward ways of your leaders who draw your country away from faith in the Lord Jesus Christ. But, what is spoken of, here, is personal repentance. You, alone in that little circle.

Do you want to speed up the coming of your ministry and that great, worldwide revival?

"...what kind of people ought you to be? You ought to live holy and godly lives as you look forward to the day of God and speed its coming." (2 Peter 3:11)

Living "holly and godly lives" involves repenting of your sins – ALL your sins. Ask the Lord to search your heart to reveal to you what you have a hard time remembering. And ask the Lord's forgiveness. Ask Him to forgive you for all the sins you cannot remember. He will forgive you. This way, when the devil reminds you of a sin you committed but have forgotten, you can just tell him, "It's under the blood of Jesus – forgiven and forgotten...no record!" The accuser has to flee:

"Submit yourselves, then, to God. Resist the devil, and he will flee from you." (James 4:7)

And while you are still in your little circle drawn on the floor, continue with **verses 8-10:**

"Come near to God and He will come near to you. Wash your hands, you sinners, and purify your hearts, you double-minded. Grieve, mourn and wail. Change your laughter to mourning and your joy to gloom. Humble yourselves before the Lord, and He will lift you up."

You may say, "Wait a minute, I'm saved, born again and baptized. I'm not that bad!"

Yes, you are saved by grace, you didn't earn it. It is a free gift **(Ephesians 2:8-9)**. Some say that you only need to be forgiven once, when you are saved. The blood of Jesus covers your past, present and future sins. I don't know about you, but I want a very personal, close relationship with my Father in heaven. When I have sinned, I go sit at His feet and pour my heart to Him and plead His forgiveness, which He gives me. He loves me and cleanses me white as snow. I want to come before Him with my sins because I love Him. Saints of God, just go by THE PLAN. Remember:

"...all have sinned and fall short of the glory of God..." (Romans 3:23)

Please spend as much time as you need in that little circle of yours. And when you have repented of all your sins and forgiven all others, and you have dried your tears, know that God has forgiven ALL your sins and there is no more remembrance of them in all of heaven.

"Though your sins are like scarlet, they shall be as white as snow; though they are red as crimson, they shall be like wool." (Isaiah 1:18)

"For I will forgive their wickedness and will remember their sins no more." (Jeremiah 31:34)

"'Their sins and lawless acts I will remember no more.'" (Hebrews 10:17)

Now that God has shown you perfect forgiveness, you, in turn, go and forgive ALL that have sinned against YOU. Yes, ALL who have stolen from you and betrayed, hurt, insulted, belittled, double crossed, cheated, injured you and lied to you. Let the devil (the accuser) have nothing against you in that part of your life and he will flee from you. Don't get out of that little circle until you have forgiven ALL. As you have been forgiven and given a clean slate, forgive and give everyone a clean slate whom YOU have forgiven. As God has forgotten your sins, then you also forget all those sins sinned against you.

Stay in that little circle for as long as it takes – days, weeks, months. It's time to clean the temple of the Lord, which you are (1 Corinthians 6:19). If you want to continue being forgiven by God, then you must forgive others:

"For if you forgive men when they sin against you, your heavenly Father will also forgive you. But if you do not forgive men their sins, your Father will not forgive your sins." (Matthew 6:14, 15)

You will know when you are ready to come out of your little circle and humbly serve the Lord in your ministry. You will have a peace which surpasses all understanding. For the joy that is set before you, you will serve the "least of these" in the name of Jesus. However, from time to time you will have to go back in that little circle for some precious alone time with Jesus to "spruce up" the temple of the Lord.

Why must you do your spiritual housekeeping before you start your ministry? Because the very thing you are doing (forgiveness), you will be ministering to others to help set THEM free from this horrible bondage. Do not be a hypocrite. Teach to the other saints of God only that which you have learned by faith.

Part 3

Get Your House In Order

As I have mentioned in Part 2 above, repentance and forgiveness are the most important aspects of cleansing the "temple" of the Lord (you). Anything within you that gets between you and the Lord must be removed; anger, bitterness, addictions, unforgiveness, jealousy, greed, bad temper, etc. Allow the fire of God to burn away the wood, hay or straw, testing the quality of your works **(1 Corinthians 3:12).** If you want to keep some of these, there will not remain a solid, powerful, lasting ministry. With God's help, you CAN be set free and cleansed, and go forth to serve the Lord more fully than ever before. Some things need to be crucified. Pray to Jesus to increase the process by which there is less of you and more of Him. Carry your daily cross.

I have mentioned the Lord gave me the word, *"Cleanse the temple of the Lord (you). Get your house in order."* Part 2 elaborated on cleansing your temple of the Lord - everything within you. Now we will discuss getting your house in order.

Getting your house in order concerns everything external to you. That is, your physical house, your friends, your family. Is the place where you live making it difficult for you to grow in your relationship with God? Do you live in an area of town where you are tempted to sin? Do you live so far from town that you are not meeting with caring saints of God? Are you living with someone you should not be? Is it time to get your house in order?

Are your friends drawing you away from the Lord Jesus Christ? Remember, you are who your friends are. You might have friends you think you can pull up to Jesus, yet they are pulling you further down into the world, instead. If you stand on a chair and try to pull someone up to stand on the chair with you, what do you think will happen? They will much more easily pull you down rather than you pull them up. It is time to get your house in order!

Is your family taken care of? Are you at peace with your family? Now is the time to settle any lingering family issues or disputes. Family may include your spouse, sons, daughters, parents, grandparents, etc.

"If anyone does not provide for his relative, and especially for his immediate family, he has denied the faith and is worse than an unbeliever." (1 Timothy 5:8)

Over the years, I have seen so many spouses, sons and daughters neglected by a father (or mother) because of zealous involvement in the Lord's ministry. Those neglectful ministers quote **Matthew 19:29** to support their negative, damaging, abusive behavior:

"And everyone who has left houses or brothers or sisters or father or mother or children or fields for my sake will receive a hundred times as much and will inherit eternal life."

The above statement Jesus made is called a hyperbole, which is an exaggeration or overstatement intended to produce an effect without being taken literally. We do that all the time: *I'm so hungry, I could eat a cow; this suitcase weights a ton; I told you a million times not to exaggerate!*

This answer from the Lord was a result of Peter's comment **(v. 27), "We have left everything to follow you!"** But had he really? Peter really didn't leave his brother, Andrew, who was with him as one of the disciples! He didn't completely leave his fishing business, as he went back to it right after Jesus' death on the cross. Also, Peter didn't leave his wife, but actually took her with him wherever he went **(1 Corinthians 9:5)**. Peter needed to make Jesus the MOST important relationship in his life.

However, Peter did "die" to the world as much as he knew how. That's the most he knew to do at that particular time. Later on, Peter was able, with the guidance of the Holy Spirit, to grow in the faith and keep his eyes on Jesus rather than on the world. And so must you in order to have a growing ministry.

After being called by God to deliver His people from Egypt, Moses had to get his house in order. He had to peacefully settle things with his father-in-law before leaving to serve in his ministry:

"Then Moses went back to Jethro his father-in-law and said to him, 'Let me go back to my own people in Egypt to see if any of them are still alive." Jethro said, "Go, and I wish you well." (Exodus 4:18)

Since Moses was going to have a ministry in Egypt, he had to get his house in order also concerning his wife and his children, whom he took along with him. However, Moses had neglected to circumcise his son which means he had neglected to teach his family the ways of the Lord, the Abrahamic Covenant.

"At a lodging place on the way (to Egypt), the Lord met Moses and was about to kill him. But Zipporah took a flint knife, cut off her son's foreskin and touched Moses' feet with it. "Surely you are a bridegroom of blood to me (because of the circumcision)," she said. So the Lord let him alone." (Exodus 4:24-26)

This was the second time God was angry at Moses and, in this instance, warned of killing him. Thank God, Moses brought his wife along with him. In fact, he also brought his brother, Aaron, and his sister, Miriam.

Saints of God, get your house in order to be released to grow in your ministry. Save yourself future problems that could destroy your ministry and hurt those you have been called to help.

Likewise, when we look at Gideon's first steps in his new ministry, we see that he had to first get his house in order before moving on to greater things. According to God's direction, he had to establish that the Lord God was the head of the family (not Baal) before starting his ministry.

"That same night the Lord said to him, 'Take the second bull from your father's herd...Tear down your father's altar to Baal and cut down the Asherah pole beside it. Then build a proper kind of altar to the Lord your God on the top of this height.'" (Judges 6:25, 26)

This caused mayhem in the village the next day. Gideon's father had to make a decision in favor of the God of Israel **(v. 31)**. Likewise, in your home, there has to be a "proper kind of altar" to the Lord which is high above everything else. If it doesn't honor God, get rid of it. Is there an offensive painting on your wall? Do you have any travel souvenirs on your mantel, like Mayan god dolls from your trip to Mexico, or Haitian voodoo dolls? How about that pornographic magazine in the closet? What needs to be removed from your house to be in order with God?

You are a work in progress, which means you will not be able to change everything overnight. Have you started to get your house in order? Have you begun cleansing the temple of the Lord? Is it your heart's desire to do this and please the Lord? If you have answered "YES" to all three questions, you may be ready to move ahead with THE PLAN.

CHAPTER eight

Feed My Sheep

Part 1

Prepare To Go In The Street

Before you proceed with the rest of these chapters, I will assume that:

1. You have spent considerable time in "your little circle" forgiving and being forgiven.
2. You are cleansing the "temple" of the Lord.
3. You are getting your house "in order."

The above three points are going to be achieved with humbleness and much patience, and this will be an ongoing process. You are always in the process of being perfected (if you are willing to grow in Christ Jesus). In fact, you will not stop being perfected until the day you die. However, do not wait until you are "perfect" to join the ministry to the "least of these." This is the devil's ruse to stop you from moving forward and effectively serving the Lord.

Even with all your faults, problems, shortcomings, doubts, sins, and other human issues, HIT THE STREET to minister in the name of Jesus Christ. You do not have guilt; you have forgiveness. At this point, you are not concerned with what is behind you, but what is ahead of you.

So, let's go in the street. It would be better if you have someone else with you. Especially someone who has been there and done it. Jesus sent His disciples two by two for good reasons – as witnesses and for mutual support. This was not just for the "Twelve." It's for you, also.

"After this the Lord appointed seventy-two others and sent them two by two ahead of him to every town and place where he was about to go." (Luke 10:1)

However, if all there is you, be of good courage and do it.

"And David was greatly distressed; for the people spake of stoning him...but David encouraged himself in the Lord his God." (1 Samuel 30:6 KJV)

Part 2

On Any Given Day

On any given day, you might decide to go bless homeless people. If you are going to minister to the homeless, BRING THEM SOMETHING. Your words to them are meaningless if you are not taking care of their basic needs.

"Suppose a brother or sister is without clothes and daily food. If one of you says to him, 'Go, I wish you well; keep warm and well fed,' but does nothing about his physical needs, what good is it? In the same way, faith by itself, if it is not accompanied by action, is dead." (James 2:15-17)

If you are going to feed the homeless, you may want to go in the late morning, right before lunch, or in the early afternoon. You may not want to go after three or four in the afternoon because some of them start to get their "drunk" on which makes communicating a little harder. The day on which you go is important because many churches or organizations in your town may feed the poor. Some only feed breakfast on Monday or Tuesday, let's say. Some will feed lunch on Monday through Friday, but not Wednesday. Others might offer dinner once or twice a week. If you plan on feeding the hungry (and minister to them), you've got to know that they are hungry!

I pray that there may be many ministries that cater to the poor and homeless in your town, whether for food, clothing, overnight stay, counseling or other ministries. At one time or another, the homeless will tell you "horrible" stories about a ministry. You, on the other hand, are NEVER to belittle any other ministries no matter who you are with at the time. Do not partake of other people's complaining about others. Remain positive, building UP the body of Christ without grumbling.

When you come to them with food, they may have just eaten. Most of the homeless eat only one meal a day. It takes too much out of them to travel from one church to another for three meals a day...if three meals can be available in one day. Try to keep track of which church feeds when. The Salvation Army, Rescue Missions, and other organizations and churches that cater to the homeless may offer meals. Most of the time, Wednesday and Sunday will most likely be hungry days because no one else may feed the homeless on those days. That's where you come in.

If you can't keep a schedule of all the feeding stops, just ask the homeless. If you ask them, they will tell you the "when", "where", and "how". And they will tell you on what day they would really like you to come. There might be a few times when you bring food for them on Wednesday or Sunday, but another benevolent person has just brought them some delicious fried chicken. Rejoice in the Lord that someone else is loving on the homeless. Do not be frustrated. Serving the Lord is not a competitive sport!

They may not want your food at this point. You'd think they would take it, but food can spoil fast and may not be worth saving. However, many of them live only for the moment and once they've eaten they are content and have no thought for tomorrow. So, go and find some others who may be hungry and feed them.

On the day that you are going to make your "rounds," get your vehicle ready. At the Rescue Mission store, you may have bought some jeans or T-shirts for them. Bring a variety of sizes. You may carry certain things with you, like white socks (which are worth their weight in gold to the homeless), nail clippers, disinfectant wipes, small flashlights, batteries (for flashlights, radio, etc.), coats, hats, gloves, scarves (in the wintertime), shorts and T-shirts (in the summer), water bottles, an assortment of books (some like to read!) You may not wish to bring all these things, but specializes in one thing or another.

Ask them what they need. Usually, it's something small and cheap to get. You would think that they would give you a long list of things they want...but they don't. Whatever they own, they have to carry with them. The less they carry, the better they can get around. If you let people know about your ministry, they may give you things for the homeless, especially clothing. You can also go to a church clothes closet or to second hand stores and pick up some things.

When it comes to food, you may bring them sweet snacks, sandwiches, fried chicken, hamburgers, bean burritos from Taco Bell, etc. The burritos run only about a buck each and they are nutritious, tasty, stick-to-your-ribs food. Bring a variety of sauces so they can have their pick. The burritos stay warm for a long time which is a plus in the winter. When you give these out in the winter, you'll find a few of the homeless just hold them for a long time before eating them because they are so warm in their hands. After you buy them, you can put them in a small icebox to keep them warm...which they do for about 2-3 hours. Some of the homeless said they had kept the burritos for up to two days before eating them - with no ill effect. This is not recommended for those who have not built up this sort of intestinal tolerance. Still, make sure the food is fresh when you pass it out.

You can go to camps where you pass out the burritos (or hamburgers, or sandwiches) and stay with the homeless a while to see what other needs they may have. You can also drive around town and stop to pleasantly surprise a homeless person with food and whatever will bless them.

You may also choose to hold church services for the homeless, with worship music, after which you can cook them a delicious spaghetti dinner with meatballs and French bread right on the spot. (How to do all this will be discussed in other chapters)

You may bring them food, clothing and other needed items. You may sit with them and chit-chat for a while. You may befriend some of them and have a great time with shared stories and adventures. All of the above are good and important, and satisfying for them and for you. All of the above do build relationship, which is important.

HOWEVER, never forget the real reason you are there. Your first and most important concern is, and always must be, their spiritual welfare.

Throughout your relationship with the homeless, you must keep your eyes on Jesus. You are "doing it to Jesus." He is the reason why you are there, in the street. Don't just spend time with them and give them "things," but forget their eternity. They are not just your friends; they are your sheep. When Jesus said to Peter, "Feed my sheep," do you think He meant, "Give them a bean burrito!" Feeding food for the stomach is important, but feeding them spiritual food is most important.

You have three main goals when ministering to the "least of these."

1. *Their salvation is first.*

Are they saved, born again, going-to-heaven Christians and do they know it without a shadow of a doubt? If you ask them if they are saved and they answer,

"I think so," your work is cut out for you. You must make their salvation SURE.

If they have not been baptized, YOU baptize them in the name of the Father, the Son and the Holy Ghost (in the pool, creek, lake, ocean)! You have authority to do that just as Jesus' disciples did **(John 4:2).**

2. *Encourage them in the Lord.*

If they are saved, remind them of how much Jesus loves them. Jesus died on the cross so that ALL their sins can be forgiven. Have a different scripture for them every time you see them. Ask if they want you to pray for them (right there and then). After a while, they will ask YOU for prayer. Leave them with a prayer and an encouraging word.

3. *Disciple them.*

Teach them how they can bring others to salvation and how they can encourage others in the Lord! It may be on a basic level, though I have seen a few of the homeless who had a shepherd's heart for the other homeless and discipleship was the next obvious step for them.

We will discuss all the different ministries available for you to minister to the "least of these." There are so many available from which to pick. There are so many needs in the street. What you may consider a minor need in your life becomes a major need in the street...like a three dollar pair of reading glasses, or a can of bug spray (summer), or underwear, or a large print New Testament.

No matter what your personality or your gifts or your preferences, there is a way for you to bless the "least of these." There is a successful way for you to bring them to salvation, encourage them in the Lord and disciple them. For all that, God has a plan.

"Each one should use whatever gift he has received to serve others, faithfully administering God's grace in its various forms...so that in all things God may be praised through Jesus Christ." (1 Peter 4:10, 11)

CHAPTER *nine*

You Are Not Alone

Part 1

Expand Your Circle

Saints of God, you have up to now spent much time with just your-self and the Lord in "your little circle," which eventually freed you from your past and brought you great peace and confidence in your Savior Jesus Christ. You have also spent some time, alone or two by two, venturing out in the streets "testing the waters," which has increased your faith in the Lord for the path He has set before you. Your heart is now burning within you, knowing that you are on the right track to serving God. You have purpose and place. It's what you have been waiting for all these years. It was that "gut feeling" you had all along inside of you. Nobody knew...but you knew.

However, saints of God, after having gone in the street to minister to God's precious children, you probably have more questions now than ever! Please, do not waste precious time re-inventing the wheel! You do not need to learn all by yourself how to minister to the "least of these." Others have gone before you; they have learned what to do, and they are more than willing to share it with you. This will save you a lifetime of learning.

According to THE PLAN of God, it is now necessary for you to expand your circle of saints of God. You are not alone in this.

God is raising a whole army! It is not God's plan for you to do this alone.

You will find out later how important is what I am going to tell you. You may not realize it at first, but all of God's little parts of His plan will fit perfectly together in the end. You will stand amazed much later on as you realize that the Sovereign God we worship has put together a plan that no man could. That's because Jesus is;

"...the Alpha and the Omega...who is and who was, and who is to come, the Almighty." (Revelation 1:8)

God is the only one who knows the whole future of humanity. Your future, rather than your past, is what truly impacts your present. In order to be where God wants you to be in the future, you must prepare now, in the present. Your past is gone, forgiven and forgotten by God, and cannot be altered in any way at all. Have faith in THE PLAN that God has for your future and move FORWARD. Do not even LOOK back (remember Lot's wife), but keep your eyes on Jesus.

"Let us fix our eyes on Jesus, the author and perfecter of our faith...so that (we) will not grow weary and lose heart." (Hebrews 12:2, 3)

The question now becomes, "Who to meet and where?" If you attend church, you may start to talk to your church family about your "ministry." They will feel your excitement and will want to ask you some questions. Invite them to come with you, one day, so that they may see for themselves (one or two at a time, of course). The Lord will add to your ministry those who are on the sidelines and are eagerly waiting to be called to active service in the Lord. Tell them about this book so they can read it and get a better idea of what you are doing (or better - give them one).

We have a brother in Christ who has been training with us now almost a year. He is a precious saint of God and has a deep burden for the homeless. Even though Dennis is on a limited disability income, he has been one of our most consistent ministers (and promising preacher to the "least of these"). His deep faith in Jesus Christ has been manifested in his ministry since the first day he has been with us.

Dennis is very vocal about his ministry to the homeless and is sharing THE PLAN that God has for His remnant. He is also actively sharing his ministry to the "least of these" on Facebook and on a website which he has created (concerned with saving souls for Christ and bringing the lost back home). Dennis did not know anything about the ministry to the homeless on day one with us. However, he is now respectfully known in the homeless circles throughout our city. We and the homeless thank God for him.

If you are not attending church, talk to family, friends, neighbors, strangers at a store - everybody! If you are going to church, talk to all the above, anyhow. It is amazing how many people God puts in your way for you to share His wonderful love and work. A simple shared testimony can put you in touch with someone whose heart was prepared by the Lord to minister to the poor. Remember, you are that spark in the street.

Start a blog, or Tweet or Facebook or start a website to let the world know about the plight of the "least of these" in your city and the Biblical references involved. Ask everyone for donations of clothing, shoes and other needed items. Others will notice your ministry once you are CONSISTENTLY operating in that ministry. People will be drawn to your "consistency" and will begin to identify you with your ministry. Be aware that not as many will join you in the street with your ministry to the "least of these" as you would hope. But many may support you by supplying you. Once you have two or three who will go in the street with you, then you have to move to the next step of THE PLAN - the home meetings.

Part 2

To Meet Or Not To Meet?

"And let us consider how we may spur one another on toward love and good deeds. Let us not give up meeting together, as some are in the habit of doing, but let us encourage one another – and all the more as you see the Day approaching." (Hebrews 10:24, 25)

You simply can't do it alone. Neither is it meant for just you and Jesus alone to do it. God does NOT want you to do it alone. Believe me, you don't want to do it alone! Of course, "it" means your ministry; the way you use your gifts to show God's love to the "least of these" in the street. If you think for one moment you want to do it alone, get back in your little circle – God wants to talk to you! Yes, we NEED Jesus, but we also NEED each other; we need "community."

Why do we need each other? Look at the above Word of God. We need each other to spur one another on. Spur, here, means to urge on; to stir up; to instigate; to cause trouble for Satan. It means that when you meet, there is a cheering section waiting for you. And after you've been cheered, then you become part of the cheerleading squad for the next saint of God. Why would you do that? Because you want to urge on and stir up one another to Godly love and good deeds, without which a ministry would be meaningless.

When you are in any sort of ministry, you WILL need encouragement. From time to time, you may be able to encourage yourself in the Lord. However, sooner or later, you will need serious encouragement from the other saints of God who understand the street ministry to the poor. You are human and you will experience human frailty. Yes, I know, "You can do all things in Christ

Jesus"... "With God all things are possible"...yet... you are still human. Part of THE PLAN of God is that He made it so we need each other. I am not being negative. Needing each other is a good thing. Saints of God, we need each other more now than ever, as the Day is approaching fast.

The church establishment only partially fulfills the requirement of "meeting together." You probably do meet in a church building of some sort, and you should. However, there has been a forsaking (giving up) of intimate meeting together. Obviously, as the above scripture shows, the first century church had a problem with people not meeting together in this manner, or else there would not have been such a warning.

Many people meeting together attracted attention and was dangerous because of the persecution of Christians at the time. Many saints met in homes in small enough numbers which would not attract attention. This was further reinforced by the destruction of the Temple by the Romans in A.D. 70. With no more "big church" to go to, the saints had to resort to smaller home meetings. It is part of God's plan.

Small home meetings have been the plan in most of the world's countries where there has been serious Christian persecution; China, Vietnam, North Korea, the Moslem countries, the former United Soviet Socialist Republic (U.S.S.R. - Russia), and too many others to list here.

I saw on the news just yesterday that a bomb exploded in a Christian church in Egypt, killing eighty-seven saints of God. That was just one of many churches that was destroyed and burned to the ground by radical Muslims in Egypt within the past six months (2013). Large churches will increasingly continue to be easy targets for the enemies of God.

After Mao Tse-Tung's communist revolution took over China in 1949, the Christian population was no longer allowed to meet in Churches. All the church buildings were confiscated and turned into government offices, museums, theatres or community centers. No Christian evangelism, worship or even singing was allowed, with bibles and hymnbooks being burned. Many Christians were persecuted and many church leaders "disappeared." The church, as such, had to go "underground;" that is, to small, personal home meetings.

It was said that under communism, the Evangelical Church in China GREW tenfold, while in the former Soviet Union the Evangelical Church SHRANK tenfold. While the former Soviet Union had some religious freedom, it was the heavily persecuted Chinese who experienced a Christian revival! The conservative Russian church was more concerned with keeping their church buildings, which they valued (if there was no church building; it was not a church); it was more concerned about SURVIVAL rather than REVIVAL. The Chinese underground church, on the other hand, had a sense of "community" (home church): they could minister through suffering; they had Chinese missionaries working in minority areas (to the "least of these"); they found ways to evangelize, disciple, and train people for ministry; and knowing the government had lied to them, they were searching for the "truth," which had to include spiritual answers.

Fifty years later, in 1999, the way was made for an increasing number of missionaries to be able to go to China, and they were very surprised. Even with serious persecution over a period of fifty years, the Christian church in Communist China had GROWN to larger numbers. Home meetings worked then and there (and still do), as they did in the first century church. God has THE PLAN. (Reference for the previous three paragraphs: John E. White, Growth Amidst Persecution, International Journal of Frontier Missiology, 29:3, Fall 2012, 139-145)

Though America's Christian church is very similar to the former Russian church, persecution is now coming mainly from attacks from the legal system (our courts and judges). It will not be long before the very loud, organized, antichrist minority will directly and physically persecute the large, visible church establishment. The fact is, that process has already begun and is speeding up. Try telling the population of the United States that marriage ordained by God is ONLY between a man and a woman, as written in the Scriptures. Or try telling the world that Jesus is the ONLY way to heaven!

The fast growing, emboldened enemy will come after you like an uncontrollable, hungry lion seeking to kill and devour you. Those who believe in same sex marriage want their freedom of expression, but will violently deny you the same right. Likewise, the radical Muslims want you to respect their religion, but will not reciprocate (that means they will not return the respect).

But rejoice, saints of God, the Lord has THE PLAN!

As you look ahead and prepare for a street ministry to the "least of these," plan now for more intimate, supportive, encouraging home meetings; find areas where the "least of these" are found; grow closer to the Lord; train and disciple others; and carry your cross. At home meetings, you will experience a community of spiritual unity to spur each other on to a greater relationship with Jesus Christ, our Lord and Savior. Glory to God!

CHAPTER *ten*

A Place For The Remnant

Part 1

A Necessity For A Powerful Ministry

My first home meeting was in 1971 at the home of Robert and Cathy Friedland in Portsmouth, Virginia (Robert's dad, also called Robert, was a Baptist pastor). I was led to a place where I was saved by Cathy, who was six years older than me. Just after I was saved, she invited me for a light dinner and fellowship with her husband and another relatively new convert. As we read the Bible, this loving couple answered many of my questions, and so much more. Then we had prayer.

Robert was a big, strong guy who played football – a man's man! However, that evening, I saw that big, burly guy get on his knees on the living room floor, by the coffee table, and offer up a most humble prayer to my new-found Lord and Savior. As a new Christian, I was awed by his humbleness. I thought if he could do it, I certainly could humble myself, also. I accepted their invitation to go to their church. I thought it would be just a larger version of this wonderful home meeting we had had.

It wasn't!

A home meeting is a place where you find intimacy with the Lord and His saints. It's where you feel comfortable enough to ask all sorts of questions you might think people at church would ridicule. Home meetings are where you can seek the Lord with heartfelt, simple worship music. There, you can first exercise your gifts, whether prophecy, teaching, music, healing, intercession, administration, organization, etc. It might be where you first pray out loud in front of people. It could be where you first lay hands on someone, and pray a prayer of healing for them. A home meeting can be a sanctuary where you can cry or laugh...or be healed. It's a place to grow together in the knowledge and love of Christ Jesus. A place to hear the gentle, loving voice of our Lord and Savior calling us to sit at His feet and have fellowship with Him.

It's part of THE PLAN of God. Of a certainty, we MUST have home meetings.

Home meetings are an important function for the saints of God who minister to the "least of these." I am not saying that you are going to bring the "least of these" to the home meetings at this time. What I am saying is that these needed, specialized home meetings are for the ministers who go out in the street to minister to the poor (to minister means to "help"). As a harvester in the field, you will need a place where you can learn to be a better harvester.

As a disciple of the Lord, you will need encouragement from time to time. You may want to have great home meetings where everyone who wants to grow in Christ can be invited. However, these meetings which I am speaking of in this book are specifically for those who will serve the poor in the street ministry. These meetings are, first of all, for the "remnant" of the faith which presently refuses to bow the knee to the gods of this world.

"I have reserved for myself seven thousand who have not bowed the knee to Baal. So too, at the present time there is a remnant chosen by grace." (Romans 11:4, 5)

Having held my own home meetings since 1982, I will testify that God has ALWAYS met us at EVERY single meeting. Though some meetings were more powerful than others, the Holy Spirit moved in all – 100% - of the meetings, and we always left better than when we came! Most of the meetings were open to everyone, whether a new convert or long-time Christian. However, recently (as directed by the Lord) we are having meetings that focus mostly on strengthening the harvesters, the ministers (helpers).

Part 2

How Often?

No matter how busy you may be, it is imperative that you take the time for regularly scheduled home meetings. You may find that having meetings during the week is almost impossible unless you give up everything else in your life. Most people work, and it is difficult getting up the next morning after a meeting that lasted until midnight the night before. We have had meetings that lasted until two in the morning! A missionary friend of mine told me they would have all night meetings when he was in Morocco. They were less visible at night than during the day, avoiding possible persecution. So, when is the best day to have a meeting (in America)?

I have tried every day of the week when I first started holding home meetings. Over the years, this is what I found; home meetings worked best on Fridays.

You can get up late on Saturday from a late Friday night meeting and still have your Saturday to "recover." For many people, Saturday morning is for chores, and the evening is the main time for rest and recreation – especially if you have a family. You also may have greater peace of mind on Friday night knowing you do not have to work the next day. Most people work from Monday to Friday, but, obviously, there are some who work on Saturday. They may want to leave the meeting early – if they can!

However, do not limit yourselves. It is completely acceptable to have a meeting on any day that works for all involved. Remain attentive to the Holy Spirit. You may want to hold meetings on Saturday or Sunday evenings (some churches have no Sunday night services). I have known saints of God who had home meetings on Wednesday nights because they were used to meeting at their church anyhow. It is whatever day your little group agrees to have a home meeting. The day to have a meeting is not written in stone.

At first, you may want to hold meetings once a month. During the rest of the month, you will have been touched by the Holy Spirit in wonderful ways, ministering in the street, relating with other saints of God, growing in the Lord, and otherwise acquiring a journal (you are writing a journal, aren't you?) full of amazing testimonies that give glory to the Father. As time passes by, you will become excited with the thought of going to a home meeting and sharing all that the Lord has done in your life during the past month. You may even want to have meetings twice a month! At one point, I have had saints of God who were so excited about the home meetings we were having, they wanted to meet every week! So we did.

However, saints of God, there is coming a time when you will want to hold home meetings every day of the week! I am telling you this as a word of prophecy, with permission from the Holy Spirit. Remember, everything God is instructing us to do is moving us in a specific direction. You will be having home meetings now in the present to help you be where God wants you in the future. God has THE PLAN.

"They all joined together constantly in prayer, along with the women and Mary the mother of Jesus, and with his brothers." (Acts 1:14)

"Every day they continued to meet together in the temple courts." (Acts 2:46)

Part 3

At What time?

The time to have a meeting is dependent on a couple of factors. First of all, it is difficult to get off work, drive home, fix dinner, eat and then drive to a meeting early enough so the meeting doesn't last past midnight. If, as most people do, you get off work at 5 pm, it would be difficult to be at a home meeting by 6:00 in the evening. What you can do to solve this dilemma, is to have everyone bring something to eat so as to have a light (quick) potluck dinner. This way the stress of fixing a meal can be eliminated and time can be saved. You can be at the meeting at 6:00, eat, clean up and be ready by the start of the meeting at 7:00.

Sharing a meal together allows for the sharing of current events - family, church, work, school, kids, etc. - and gets those subjects out of the way by the time it's time to start the meeting. Sharing a pot-luck dinner is comforting, and you will find yourself more relaxed when finished with the meal than when you arrived.

After the meal, all present can then share Holy Communion as a transition to a meeting focused on the Holy Spirit. ANYONE CAN ADMINISTER HOLY COMMUNION! It does not take a priest, pastor or preacher for the "Eucharist." You can each say a prayer or share a comment as you all share the wine (grape juice) and bread (I use unleavened, whole wheat tortillas cut in pieces!) I have vivid memories of meetings with such a sweet spirit of unity and love. This godly attitude predisposes (prepares) you to be receptive to wonderful moves of the Holy Spirit in your meetings.

"...judge for yourselves what I say. Is not the cup of thanksgiving for which we give thanks a participation in the blood of Christ? And is not the bread that we break a participation

in the body of Christ? Because there is one loaf, we, who are many, are one body, for we all partake of the one loaf." (1 Corinthians 10:15-17)

Do you have to have a meal? Not at all. It all depends on the makeup of those who will attend. If they are single, then that somewhat simplifies things. But if the saints of God who are coming to the meeting are married or married with children, then that's a whole other story. Having been there myself, I can understand that this makes it a little more difficult to manage time. Hold a discussion at your first meeting on how you want to proceed – with or without a light meal. However, do try to have Holy Communion.

Notice I mention "a light meal." Anything more involved will add more time to the meeting. The main object of the meeting is to get to God's business and glorify God – not have one long meal. If you want a nice long meal, then plan on it at another time. Remember, the purpose of the meeting; testimony, training, prayer. This subject of a meal is not written in stone, so it can be subject to change as the meetings evolve.

Though home meeting meals are scriptural, Paul chastised the Corinthians' home meeting meals because they were not done in love, unity and unselfishness:

"When you come together, it is not the Lord's Supper you eat, for as you eat, each of you goes ahead without waiting for anybody else. One remains hungry, another gets drunk." (1 Corinthians 11:20-22)

"So then, my brothers, when you come together to eat, wait for each other." (1 Corinthians 11:33)

"Whether you eat or drink or whatever you do, do it all for the glory of God." (1 Corinthians 10:31)

Part 4

Miscellaneous

1. How many people should I have at a home meeting?

You should not have more than twelve people. With over twelve people, it becomes less intimate and personal. It is more difficult to have guided learning, prayer and question-and-answer sessions. It is also harder on the host and on the home. With too many people in a home, things can get broken or messy real quick. Parking in front of the home or apartment could raise the ire of neighbors. If it is found that you are having Christian home meetings, it might be construed as "having church." If a complaint is filed, zoning laws could be enforced that would prevent you from having "church" in an area which is not zoned as such. That can be a mess! Don't go there. Maximum - twelve. There are reasons why Jesus had TWELVE disciples!

When you reach twelve attendees at your meetings, then it is time to split into two groups. It will not be easy because you have been meeting for some time and now feel comfortable with each other. Some may resist this move, but it is a necessary part of God's plan. It must be discussed thoroughly at home meetings that this is what will (and must) happen. Do not just spring it on everyone one day. Discuss it as part of God's plan. Decide amongst yourselves who goes where. The split groups with only six saints of God will grow again, and everyone will be the better for it. This plan of God cannot spread if you do not split the meetings.

Do not start thinking that the solution is to get a bigger building! That is an error the church has been doing for almost two thousand years. God's plan involves decentralizing how we serve the Lord. Jesus said, "Go into all the world." He did not say, "Build bigger churches." The next great move of God (revival) will not come out of the church, but out of the street, as it did with Jesus. The "last" revival will come as did the "first" revival - in the street.

Therefore, after your meetings have reached twelve saints of God, don't be afraid to split. Have faith that God will grow you again and again and again until the whole world has been touched by a revival that sprang from ministering to the "least of these," and spread like wildfire.

2. How to dress at meetings.

Casual dress is good. If you are coming straight from your place of work and are dressed in business casual, then so be it. That's acceptable. What is not acceptable are shorts that are too short - for either men or women. In fact, there should be no shorts worn unless you are in a hot, humid tropical area, and there is no air conditioning. There is nothing more distracting than seeing "too much" when someone is sitting opposite you. Same for ladies wearing scanty tops, spaghetti straps, etc. Wear modest apparel befitting the ministers of the Lord Jesus whom you are.

3. How to address the subject of children.

If all present at the meeting have children, then hire a babysitter for your meeting. All the kids can go in a room, garage or outdoors and have activities if they are of age. Sooner or later young children allowed to stay with mom or dad will disrupt the meeting. This could turn meetings into unpleasant experiences. Some may not come back; not to mention that it breaks the continuity of prayer or teaching. It will distract from the purpose of the meeting. It is best if mom or dad have a babysitter to take care of the kids at home. You may dearly love children, but the facts are the facts.

4. Telephones.

TURN THEM OFF! If you have children at home or are in a position to receive an important call, put the phone on vibrate. When it rings (vibrates), quietly go into another room (or outside) to take the call, as long as your conversation is not overheard. That is part of being loving and considerate of others.

There is nothing worse than being with the saints of God in deep prayer and worship, seeking the Lord with all your heart and interceding with tears flowing freely...and a phone rings loudly with an annoying little worldly tune like "Wooly Bully!"

CHAPTER *eleven*

Home Meeting Primer

Part 1

Who's In Charge?

"Again, I tell you that if two of you on earth agree about anything you ask for, it will be done for you by my Father in heaven. For where two or three come together in my name, there am I with them." (Matthew 18:19, 20)

According to the above scripture, when you gather together for a home meeting, Jesus is present. As you open the meeting, make sure that you are all in unity, that you all agree as to what you want to ask the Lord; for what you are seeking Him. Though at your meeting there is only one person in charge (that is Jesus), you are nevertheless able **"by prayer and petition, with thanksgiving (to) present your requests to God." (Philippians 4:6).**

However, Jesus is not at your meeting simply to listen in and see what you are doing and give you whatever you want. Jesus Christ is the administrator; the leader of your meetings. The Holy Spirit is in charge. It is not the people present at the meeting who should say, "Come, Holy Spirit." God forbid! There is nothing in the Scriptures to support this erroneous (very wrong) position of humans commanding the Holy Spirit. Instead, it is the Holy

Spirit that says to you, "Come, saints of God." In other words, the Holy Spirit is not our servant. Rather, we are servants to the Holy Spirit, to Jesus, to the Lord our God, the One whom we glorify.

"'Lord, if it's you,' Peter replied, 'tell me to come to you...'" (Matthew 14:28)

In the above scripture, Peter did not say, "Come to me, Jesus, so I can walk on the water!" Peter instead said, "Tell me to come to you..." If it is God's will for you to do something for Him, Jesus is present. If you do not have Holy Spirit guidance to do something, you can call the Holy Spirit to come down all you want, it's not going to happen. When Peter did try to tell Jesus what to do, he was corrected somewhat harshly by Jesus:

"Get behind me, Satan! You are a stumbling block to me; you do not have in mind the things of God, but the things of men." (Matthew 16:23)

If at a meeting you have to say, "Come, Holy Spirit," then I have to ask you, "What spirit was there before you asked the Holy Spirit to come?" If you are saved, you have the indwelling of the Holy Spirit in you. Therefore, if you are present at a meeting, so is the Holy Spirit.

"...he (the Father) will give you another Counselor to be with you forever – the Spirit of truth...he lives with you and will be in you...On that day you will realize that I am in my Father, and you are in me, and I am in you." (John 14:16, 17, 20)

Remember, God will always move you "forward." He will not let you stay in one place too long ("place" here means a spiritual level of understanding). Jesus wants you to grow in the knowledge of Him. He knows where you personally need to grow, and He knows in which direction your home meetings need to go.

I must mention here, saints of God, that the purpose of the home meeting is NOT to form a "church;" no matter how enjoyable, or how popular or how blessed your home meetings may be. Do you want to forsake the intimacy and fruitfulness of small home meetings in order to sit again within the four walls of a "church?" No matter how many people want to form their "own" church; that is NOT the purpose of home meetings. Do not go there at this time. Period.

God's understanding is NOT limited. If you listen to God and let the Holy Spirit lead your home meeting, then your ministry to "the least of these" will move forward to a greater level than you could have ever managed yourself. God has THE PLAN. Listen to Him. He WILL guide your meetings. From experience I can say, "I guarantee it!"

I have found that when two saved human beings are together, you have two "denominations;" two ways of thinking! If you have twenty Christians together, you may just have twenty different "denominations." Nobody fully agrees on all that is found in the Bible. That is because our understanding is limited. Saints of God, you are not going to home meetings to find your differences, but to find your common ground; how to better glorify God in unity and love for one another.

When you come to a meeting, you have NO denomination. Denomination is demonization - conquer and divide. Denomination is abomination. Why? Because denomination is manmade. It is a curse mankind has inflicted upon itself because of its own pride. Please, saints of God, understand that denomination is NOT of God. When He comes back to get His bride, will he find her pure and holy? Or will He find her broken into many different pieces - fragmented?

We must prepare by coming into complete unity. This is one prophecy Jesus has given us that has not come to pass. And yet, it must come to pass concerning His Bride before the Lord's return. Over the past centuries, the Christian church has so easily let the devil divide the church in order to conquer it. The remnant which is rising up in our day must work in unity and in love to speed the coming of the Lord.

"May they be brought to complete unity to let the world know that you sent me and have loved them even as you have loved me." (John 17:23)

"A new command I give you: Love one another. As I have loved you, so you must love one another. By this all men will know that you are my disciples, if you love one another." (John 13:34)

You must come to your home meetings in unity of purpose with the love of God in your heart for one another. If you can't do that, then the meeting is a good place to ask the Lord to teach you unity and love. God will gladly give such things to those who ask of him. At home meetings, learn how you can make yourself ready for the Lord's coming. What do the Scriptures tell you about how Jesus will find His bride when He returns to get her?

"Let us rejoice and be glad and give him glory! For the wedding of the Lamb has come, and his bride has made herself ready. Fine linen, bright and clean, was given her to wear." (Revelation 19:7, 8)

"You ought to live holy and godly lives as you look forward to the day of God and speed its coming...So then, dear friends, since you are looking forward to this, make every effort to be found spotless, blameless and at peace with Him." (2 Peter 3:11)

Nowhere in the Word of God does it say that you have to be of the right denomination. As the end comes nearer and clearer, you must become more united, more loving, more forgiving, and ready to carry your daily cross. Do not let your home meetings become a place where you argue about who is right or wrong on this or that scripture. This is no time to be offended! You are having home meetings to move you and your ministry forward in the Name of Jesus.

"I appeal to you, brothers, in the name of our Lord Jesus Christ, that all of you agree with one another so that there may be no divisions among you and that you may be perfectly united in mind and thought." (1 Corinthians 1:10)

When you go in the street to minister to the poor, you do not go in your own name; you do not go in the name of your church; you do not go in the name of your denomination; you do not go in the name of your ministry. You go in the Name of God the Father, His Son Jesus Christ and in the power of the Holy Spirit. When the homeless ask you, "What church are you from?" You answer, "I don't come in the name of any church. I come in the name of the Lord Jesus Christ, the only name on Earth by which a man can be saved!" Glory to God! Blessed are those who are invited to the wedding supper of the Lamb!" **(Revelation 19:9).**

The Moderator

Since the Holy Spirit will lead your meetings, all you need is a "moderator" to keep things moving smoothly. The moderator makes sure that everyone gets a chance to speak. If someone speaks for too long, the moderator makes sure other people are also able to share what the Lord has put on their heart. The moderator is not the one to continually speak, teach, preach or lead the meeting.

Everyone has a gift from God to be used at meetings. The moderator makes sure everyone has a chance for their gift to be used of the Lord. Some saints can remember scriptures and where they are found. Some hear the Lord and are sensitive to the Holy Spirit. Some are intercessors or have the gift of discernment. Some are teachers or worshippers. The moderator makes sure all have a chance to voice what the Holy Spirit is saying through them. There is more than one way the Holy Spirit can speak to you. Do not let one person take over the meeting. Once the Holy Spirit gives your meeting a "direction," the moderator keeps everyone on that subject and moving in that same direction. The Holy Spirit is never wrong.

The moderator must be patient, soft spoken, loving, understanding, able to hear the Lord or be receptive to the Holy Spirit. He must be humble, not a beginner in the faith, having a grasp of the Scriptures. He must be given to the development of the gifts in the saints of God. He must carry his cross. He cares more about others than he does about himself.

You will find that once you have a good moderator, everyone will look to him to moderate at all the meetings. However, others can be given a chance to moderate. It's what you agree on and how the Holy Spirit leads. Therefore, do know who the moderator is before the meeting starts, as he will guide you through the three parts of a home meeting:

1. Testifying
2. Training
3. Praying

Part 2

Testifying

You are finally sitting down to business in someone's home (NOT a room in a church building, hotel room or commercial location, thus forsaking the warmth of a home). Dinner, if you've shared one, is over and all cleaned up. You may have taken communion together. Or, you may all just have come in out of the cold and sat down ready to go on with the meeting. There is a short prayer asking for the Holy Spirit to use anyone in the meeting as

He would, and to guide the meeting so God may get all the glory, honor and praise.

Now, brothers and sisters, it's time to testify!

The moderator starts by asking if anyone has a testimony to share. Most of the time, someone has already started because they have been keeping that testimony bottled up all week long, and they are ready to let it out. Let everyone share. If one takes much too long talking, the moderator thanks that person, then looks at brother Bob and gently says, "How about you, brother Bob? Tell us how the Lord is working in your life and ministry." You might hear confirmation of the testimony by someone else who has had the same experience. The subject of that experience may be the direction the Holy Spirit may want you to take. Remain sensitive to the Teacher.

Sister Mary was very excited to share that one of the homeless men had a nasty, open sore, and she asked him if she could pray for his healing. She saw him two times in a week (to help with antibiotic ointment and bandaging) and the third time he stopped HER and asked her to pray for him because he was getting much better. Now, the men in that group ask her to pray for them every time she is there to minister to them with food or clothing. Praise the Lord! Glory to God!

On the other hand, the testimony from Bob was that he asked a homeless man where his camp was; where he was staying at night. The homeless man suddenly stopped talking and left. Bob is not having many positive results as to where these men are staying. You see, he wants to minister to many at a time in the camps (not all homeless stay in a camp with others). Bob has been going in the street for only one month, and this is his first home meeting.

Then someone else (if not the moderator) will tell him that the homeless are suspicious of people asking them such questions. Night time is a vulnerable time for the homeless, as they can get robbed or beaten more easily when it's dark. So they get paranoid when you ask them such question. However, after a while (weeks, months) of consistently ministering to them, they will come to trust you and even ask you to come to their camp to minister to all. So now, Bob has learned something.

Because of everyone sharing what THEY do in the street, ALL present at the meeting learn what to do or not to do. Testimony is important because it causes the body of Christ to grow in a greater proportion than the people present. By the personal testimony of a few, all can grow in the ministry and in Christ. By this knowledge, the group becomes stronger than the sum of its members. That's how the Holy Spirit works!

The Holy Spirit uses one person to share a little something, and the whole body grows by it. It is not simply that person sharing, but the Holy Spirit working through that saint of God. It's a "Wow" moment, or an "Ah-ha" experience. It's confirmation to you that the Master is teaching you. Give honor to God, where honor is due. At this point, the worshippers light up. The intercessors pray for more of that Holy Spirit touch. The teacher is already putting a lesson together for that. The Scripture person has already found scripture to support that position. The moderator is allowing each in turn to speak their heart. Multiply that by how many testimonies? The meeting is on!

Support the person giving a testimony. Make fun of no one, but do laugh together! Insult or belittle no one, but gently encourage a saint of God to build them up. Don't be afraid to respectfully ask questions. Tell them how you enjoyed their testimony and how it ministered to you. Do share with them if the same thing happened to you. If someone is too quiet, lovingly coax (but do not force) them to share a little something to help them grow in Holy Spirit confidence. Love one another and remain in Godly unity.

That's why I said earlier; you cannot do this ministry alone. You need the testimony of others to help you learn and grow. Do not reinvent the wheel again. It's already been invented! YOU also need to be coaxed, encouraged, loved and hear the gentle voice of the Holy Spirit through others. And, yes, YOU also need to share with others because YOU have something to testify about that will build up the other saints of God. You need the knowledge which the Holy Spirit has hidden in your brothers and sisters in Christ.

"But we have this treasure in jars of clay to show that this all-surpassing power is from God and not from us." (2 Corinthians 4:7)

"As iron sharpens iron, so one man sharpens another." (Proverbs 27:17)

Part 3

Training

It is difficult to separate testifying from training. They are both so tied together.

After everyone has had a chance to testify, the moderator then repeats what has been learned. For example:

1. We can help the homeless with antibiotic ointment and bandages to help them heal. However, also pray for them, as their spiritual health is most important.

2. Do not ask them directly where their camp is located. Rather, ask a more gentle and caring question, "Do you have a safe place to sleep at night?" In time, if you are consistent in your love for them, they will share more of their life with you. One day, they will let you hold services in their camp. Their relationship with Christ is most important.

Then the moderator may ask, "What else did we learn from the testimonies?" The moderator may not remember all that was said (note taking is all right). Also, the moderator must resist the temptation to speak for too long. Involve others in the conversation.

So now, we make the transition to the training segment of the home meeting. This may be something that is planned if there is something new and important to discuss. The moderator may just go with the flow, keeping in mind that the Holy Spirit is guiding and in charge of the meeting. The moderator may ask what you are all doing out there, in the street that has worked.

That's where Dennis says that he makes sandwiches for the homeless. He waits until he gets in town, finds a park, sits at a picnic table and makes the peanut butter and jelly sandwiches right there. This way they are fresher than if he had made them at home (he lives far away). Then he drives to the homeless camp and passes the fresh sandwiches out to them. Sylvia then asks if there is a law against fixing food for the homeless. The laws are discussed. No, you can't prepare food yourself unless you are licensed. However, that is hardly an issue unless you are fixing a seven course meal on the sidewalk!

Then Bill comes up with what he does. In a plastic bag, he puts one jar of peanut butter, one jar of jelly, a big box of butter crackers, three plastic knives (or spoons) and a bottle of water. This way they can carry this with them and fix their own whenever they are hungry. He always carries some pre-made bags in his car and gives them out whenever he sees a homeless person. Someone asks, "Why crackers?" Because they don't go bad like a loaf of bread does.

Oh!

What do you all do about food for the homeless? What else could we do? How could we do it better? Can we have a BBQ for them? How about a spaghetti dinner? If food happens to be the direction the meeting is going for now, go with it. However it could be any subject, or multiple subjects, as all saints of God may offer something different to the homeless. There are so many ministries possible that you could talk until midnight about what can be done in the street and still touch but a fraction of it.

That's training.

How do you lead someone to salvation? Is love a gift? How can I love more? Who can tell me the difference between psychosis and neurosis in the homeless? What services are available in town for the homeless? How do we prepare to serve them this coming winter? Could someone who is rich, but mourning the loss of a loved one, be considered the "least of these?" Does anyone know a good source of cheap gloves, socks? A homeless man asked me if we are as righteous as Jesus is. Are we? How do you hold a "service" outdoors for the homeless? If the scriptures tell me not to test the Lord, then why does The Lord say in Malachi 3:10, "Test me in this?" If Jesus said you must "hate the world," why does it say in John 3:16, "For God so loved the world...?" Why did Jesus touch the leper, though it was against the "law" to touch them? Did Jesus sin by breaking the law?

We never run out of things to learn in training, whether practical or scriptural. However, everything must be supported with scripture. All that you do MUST be scripturally based. Also, you must abide by the laws of the land and plan all events with respect to all parties involved. The Lord is central to all that you do because the homeless' SPIRITUAL HEALTH IS FIRST AND FOREMOST, AND THE END GOAL OF ALL THAT YOU DO FOR THEM. The moderator must never let you forget that.

Prepare for a home meeting, but do not over prepare. It's O.K. to bring preplanned questions, concerns and even activities with you to a meeting. However do not over plan the meeting. Relax, plan on laughing, or crying, with everyone free to share without being ridiculed. You can even wear your casual "sweats" to the meeting. This is not a meeting where you have to make motions, second them, vote, with minutes, etc. Most of all, be receptive to the Lord's guidance. Do not be a clock watcher. Let the meeting flow as it will. Whether someone is rich or poor, has a great job or not; all of that is of no consequence. Treat everyone at the meeting as brothers and sisters, and as saints of God who will all walk together on streets of gold one day.

"My brothers, as believers in our glorious Lord Jesus Christ, don't show favoritism. Suppose a man comes into your meeting wearing a gold ring and fine clothes, and a poor man in shabby clothes also comes in. If you show special attention to the man wearing fine clothes and say, "Here's a good seat for you," but say to the poor man, "You stand there" or "Sit on the floor by my feet," have you not discriminated among yourselves and become judges with evil thoughts?

Listen, my dear brothers: Has not God chosen those who are poor in the eyes of the world to be rich in faith and to inherit the kingdom he promised those who love him? But you have insulted the poor." (James 2:1-6)

Part 4

Praying

"The end of all things is near. Therefore be clear minded and self-controlled so that you can pray. Above all, love each other deeply..." (1 Peter 4:7, 8)

Do not do not get carried away with the testifying and training sections of the meeting, and leave only five minutes at the end of the meeting for a quick prayer. No, no, no, saints of God! Praying is of utmost importance, even more important than the first two sections of the meeting. At a given time, the moderator must stop the motivating training section and transfer to prayer time. There might not be any smooth way of transferring from training to praying. It might be as abrupt as the moderator saying, "Well, folks, this might now be a good time to go into prayer."

The meeting should have equal time in testifying, training and prayer. If you are having a three hour meeting, then you will spend an hour in each section. Is this chiseled in stone? No! I can't say it enough, "The Holy Spirit will guide you." However, do not shortchange praying. If anything, praying will be the longest section.

It is not within the scope of this book to offer you a theological dissertation (an extended formal writing for a doctoral candidate) on effective Christian prayer. Hundreds of books have been written by man to cover the subject. My suggestion is that you would need to get your concordance out (an indispensable big book with every word used in the Bible) and look up everywhere these words appear in the Old and New Testament; pray, praying, prayed, prayer, prayers, supplication, request, and any other words that have to do with prayer. This could be studied during the training sections.

The moderator might ask, "What are some of the things we need to pray for?" The saints will call out some things that are important to them. "Remember to pray for those needs."

Whether you pray out loud or to yourself is up to you. However, do not pray so loud as to disrupt the continuity of prayer. This is not the time to be theatrical, make a show or speak in tongues loudly. Let your humble prayers be from the heart, being totally honest with the Lord. You don't even have to pray out loud, as the Lord can read your mind - you can "think" your prayers to Him. He will still hear you loud and clear!

"And when you pray, do not keep on babbling like pagans, for they think they will be heard because of their many words. Do not be like them, for your Father knows what you need before you ask him." (Matthew 6:7)

Some may want to stay in their seat, some may want to kneel or sit on the floor. Some are walkers and will need a place to stand and walk around as they seek the Lord. Do not interrupt praying with testifying or training - you've already done that. This is about praying.

At this point, music would be nice. Does someone have a guitar, a piano, a keyboard, a flute? If there is no instrument, then have an iPod on speakers or a CD? You can all sing together, as you pray, if someone is playing an instrument. Worship is part of praying. There are times when you might have ten minutes of prayer and two hours of worship. Sometimes you will have ten minutes of worship and two hours of crying before the Lord with your face to the floor, making intercession for a serious issue. Music must be suitable for prayer - not loud or challenging. This may be a good time to have quiet, instrumental sound only. Let the Holy Spirit guide you.

Prayer is boldly stepping into the Holiest and humbly coming at the feet of Jesus. Prayer is bowing down before Him with your tears washing the nail scars on His feet. Prayer is also gazing into His eyes and letting His love saturate every part of your being. Prayer is not about how much you want from the Lord, but yielding to what Jesus wants of you. Prayer is obedient submission to the Holy Spirit. Prayer is thanking God for all the good things and bad things in your life; good things because they come from God; bad things because they make you stronger. Prayer is trusting Jesus and not being afraid. Praying is asking for and believing in the impossible. Prayer is resting in the amazing power and splendor of the Lord our God. Prayer is complete surrender to His plan for your life. Prayer is about glorifying the Holy Name of Jesus Christ with all of your strength, mind, soul and heart.

Then, the Lord will say, "Ask what you will, and I will do it, that you may bear fruit and glorify the Holy Father."

"If you remain in me and my words remain in you, ask whatever you wish, and it will be given you. This is to my Father's glory, that you bear much fruit, showing yourselves to be my disciples." (John 15:7, 8)

"You did not choose me, but I chose you and appointed you to go and bear fruit - fruit that will last. Then (so that) **the**

Father will give you whatever you ask in my name. This is my command: Love each other." (John 15:16, 17)

"Do not be anxious about anything, but in everything, by prayer and petition, with thanksgiving, present your requests to God. And the peace of God, which transcends all understanding, will guard your hearts and your minds in Christ Jesus." (Philippians 4:6, 7)

Prayer time will usually wind down on its own. The moderator must be sensitive to those praying, but at one point he may have to sit down, open the Bible, or get a drink of water or some other action that gently lets others know that prayer time is winding down. Maybe he could turn the music down, and then off. Do not be abrupt, at this point, as this may be a tender moment.

This is now a time when you sit back down together and ask what the Lord has shown you. The prophets will share what the Lord has given them (this is not just restricted to prophets). Ask, "What has the Lord revealed to us; what is He telling us? How did you pray? What have you received from the Lord?" Check all answers with the scriptures. You may have a brief period of discussion as to how the Holy Spirit moved during prayer. If you received a word from the Lord, then make sure it is written down for future reference and confirmation.

Before the meeting is dismissed, have personal prayer for those who need it. Do any need healing, financial, family or any other prayer? Another option, especially for new Christians, is to one by one take turns at a short prayer. Just go clockwise until everyone has had a turn at praying. The moderator will let them know, "I'll start and then we'll move clockwise as you take your turn praying."

If one is through praying and the next one does not pray, just softly say, "Bob, it's your turn." Do not push or insist if Bob shakes his head no. He may not be ready to pray publicly. Just move to the next person. This helps the newer saints of God who are not used to praying in public. You will be praying for the homeless and the poor in public, so home meetings are a good place to practice.

Concerning the long-time Christians, it may be difficult to STOP them from long prayers out loud. Make your prayers short. Truly, nobody remembers long prayers. This is where the more you say, the less you mean! The homeless attention span for prayer is about fifteen seconds. Practice praying at home to get an idea how long is fifteen seconds. Any more than that becomes meaningless. Pray for fifteen SECONDS then let them know that you will pray for them from time to time during the coming week until you see them again. Then, when you are at home, pray your long, heartfelt prayer before the Lord. And the Lord, who can handle long prayers, will hear you.

If someone is going on and on with loud prayer, it would not be rude for the moderator to interrupt with, "Thank you, Forte, for that wonderful prayer. May God bless you with a powerful answer." The moderator then goes on with a short prayer of thanks or moves on with the subject at hand. If Forte insists on praying longer, stop him again and explain why long prayers at home meetings and in the street are meaningless. Human attention span is much shorter than God's attention span.

If you are seriously praying to the Lord for direction and knowledge, everyone will be praying - maybe not loudly. Each will be praying quietly or silently, or singing, or worshipping, or seeking and reading scriptures to themselves to seek answers from the Lord. God gives you the answer to your prayers in various ways. It may be through a song, or a scripture, or a word of knowledge, or..? Remain sensitive to the Lord and respectful of each other. Also remember, God does have a sense of humor concerning your answers to prayers!

On the other hand, if you are praying - making unified intercession - for a particular problem or issue, it may get louder as you all pour out your soul before the Lord for a spiritual and powerful breakthrough. There is nothing silent about crying before the Lord! "Crying before the Lord" is not popular in America.

However, it is done considerably more in countries where Christian persecution exists. It will become more needful and prevalent in America, as time goes on!

"Put on sackcloth, O priests (YOU are now such priests, Revelation 1:6, 5:10, 20:6)**, and mourn; wail, you who minister before the altar. Come, spend the night in sackcloth, you who minister before my God..." (Joel 1:13)**

"'Even now,' declares the Lord, 'return to me with all your heart, with fasting and weeping and mourning.'" (Joel 2:12)

CHAPTER *twelve*

Dare To Go Beyond The Church

Part 1

A Special Identity

So far, it was confirmed to you that you were born for a Godly purpose and that Jesus is the one who sends, trains, ordains and anoints you. You have found out it is OK to want to be like Jesus. You have learned how to "see" the invisibles - the poor and homeless. You have also been introduced to THE PLAN which God has for ministering in the street, leading to an unsurpassed, ground roots revival

You are in the process of getting your house in order and cleansing the "temple" of the Lord. It is hoped that you have spent some time in your "little circle," where you gave it all to the Lord, and where you will continue to give it all to Him. Then you stepped into a wider "circle" at home meetings to help you grow. You learned about testimony, training and prayer. It is hoped you have searched the scriptures, and are increasingly learning how to pray according to God's will.

It is now time to widen your "circle" to the next level. Widening your "circle" will undoubtedly involve more people in your life. Remember that when you need to, you can always go back and spend some time in your "little circle." In fact, you will need to. It's your sanctuary where you can personally touch bases with Jesus. You will also have your home meeting "circle" to strengthen and encourage you.

If you haven't already, now is the time to go beyond the church; that is, out of the church walls and into the street. Now you can go to the "least of these" with not only something in your heart, but also something in your hand. But what to bring in your hand that will bless the poor, the homeless? Can simply giving them a few dollars show your Godly love for them. If you give them money, will they have an overflowing love for you that will allow you to give them the Word of God? (The answer is, "No!")

Food is always needed. So, always bring food with you (especially high carbohydrate foods which they love; candy bars, apple and cherry pies, snacks).

However, what is most needed is to know what their particular, individual needs are. For example, I know a man who lives under a bridge who has a little cooking stove and a pan. I picked up in conversation that he loves Kielbasa sausage but can't get it. The next week I visited him, I brought him a package of Kielbasa sausage. You should have seen that man's countenance light up! You would have thought I had just given him a million dollars. He was all smiles. I knew his personal need because I empathized with him. I felt his pain. I loved him in the name of Jesus. More than that...I gave JESUS some great sausage.

A wife comes to her husband and tells him, "I would really love some flowers, Honey." So the husband looks at her, smiles, gives her his credit card and proudly says, "Here, Sweetheart, get yourself some." Do you think this husband has loved his wife? Has he acted "as unto the Lord?" God forgive him! Hear me, saints of God, "If you have done it to the least of these...you have done it to me," says the Lord Jesus Christ **(Matthew 25:40).**

Do you casually want to slip Jesus a couple of dollars? Or do you want to find what pleases Him and give Him that which he yearns for from you? Give to the homeless as if you were giving to Jesus. And never tire of it.

Once in a while, there was this slightly overweight, middle aged lady who would walk down the street by my house. She would make her way very slowly down the sidewalk, stopping here and there, looking at all the butterflies, flowers, birds, trees, all the while singing out loud (as a five year old would). Every time a car would go by, she would stop what she was doing, wave at them and loudly proclaim, "I love you, I love you!" Once the car was out of sight, she would resume her fairyland walk.

I would look at her, thinking that she was really off her rocker! Boy, this black lady was crazy. Day after day she would walk by, though if I was working outside I could hear her singing long before I could see her. Obviously, she did have some "issues," but she did no one any harm. I found no reason to go out there and speak to her.

"He who mocks the poor shows contempt for their Maker;" (Proverbs 17:5)

Then one night I had a dream. In the dream, the Lord says to me, concerning this particular woman, "I sent you an angel to see if you would entertain her. And you did not."

Oh no! I had let Jesus down. The fear of the Lord gripped me! I woke up and immediately got on my knees and begged God's forgiveness. I asked Jesus to please send her down my street one more time that I may love her in His Holy Name, for she was one of the "least of these."

The very next day, there she comes down the road singing. I immediately went outside to intercept her and find out about her. She saw me coming, waved at me with both hands, and started her routine, "I love you, I love you!" I was wondering where she was coming from, that she walks in front of my house every day.

She answered in her simple way, "I just came from church."

"What did you do there?" I asked doubting her, since this was not a "church" day.

Her joyful reply, spoken through ill-fitting dentures, was, "I volunteer for three hours a day. Sometimes I answer the phone, 'Hello, this is ---- Church, can I help you?' But mostly I help hand out food to the poor that come to the church in the morning."

Then she added, "I walk two and a half miles to church and two and a half miles back home."

I wanted to cry. I had judged this lady, and of course I had judged her wrong. She was a beautiful little child of God. I asked her what her name was. Mary...like the mother of Jesus.

I gave Mary a ride home. She rented a room in an old, wooden home. I asked her why she did not take the bus which ran exactly where she was going.

"Don't have no money," she said plainly.

The next day, as she came down the street, I called out to her, "Mary, come here. I've got something for you." I had a five dollar bill in my hand. "I want you to have this so you can take the bus."

She crossed the street towards me so fast her wig almost fell off. Her eyes became as big as saucers, and she had a smile so big I thought her dentures would fall out. She came to me, giving me a big 'ol sweaty bear hug from a bear who would not let go.

She ignored the five dollar bill.

Still hugging me, she exclaimed, with tears in her eyes, "You remembered my name! Mary. You remembered my name! Nobody remembers my name. Nobody remembers me. But you remembered my name! I love you! I love you! And now I know that you love me. Oh, bless you in the name of Jesus." The earnest hugging would not stop.

I still minister to Mary, from time to time, and I still get Mary hugs. However, sometimes I think she ministers more to me.

The most you can do, sometimes, is to remember their names. It is one way to preserve human dignity in the midst of poverty. Remember the names of all the poor and homeless to whom you minister. Period. Using their name often when you speak to them shows that you have esteem (means great value; appreciation or respect) for them. If you must, carry a small pad of paper and a pen to take notes in the street. Their name is a special identity God has given them. God knows all His children intimately by name.

"A good name is more desirable than great riches; to be esteemed is better than silver or gold." (Proverbs 22:1)

Part 2

Your Neighborhood

Mary lives within half a mile from my house. That half-mile circle is my neighborhood. Your neighborhood circle may be smaller or bigger, depending on where you live. If you live in the worst, poorest part of town, your needy neighborhood circle may be a quarter of a mile, or even just blocks. If you live in a very nice subdivision, you may have to go farther out to find the "least of these." Your neighborhood "circle" might be a mile, or even more.

You may not live in a city or town or even near a town. You may live in the countryside where you are already more likely to understand how to give to a neighbor in need. Either way, you could spend the rest of your life ministering to the least of these just in your neighborhood which would result in your neighborhood revival!

Listen to me, saints of God, and believe what I am saying to you. This is part of THE PLAN of God for this ministry. Your ministering to the poor and homeless MUST FIRST START IN YOUR NEIGHBORHOOD CIRCLE. I am giving you the truth.

When I tell you, "This is part of THE PLAN of God," please know that I have not decided this by myself just yesterday! I have challenged it, prayed over it, searched the scriptures, and waited patiently (but mostly impatiently). I sought confirmation of what

God was giving me wherever God would give it. Many nights were spent in prayer; many days in fasting, alone or with others. Years have gone by before I am finally able, by permission from the Lord, to present this to you. In fact, the Holy Spirit is now urging me on, as the return of our Lord Jesus Christ draws near.

I have no ulterior (hidden) or self-serving motives in telling you this or in writing this book. My number one motive is to glorify our Savior, Jesus Christ, as we prepare His bride (the saved) for His coming, according to His plan. Many saints of God have a part in THE PLAN of God. This is my part. Glory to God!

THE PLAN of God was put to the church, to the saints, to the street, and I suffered and agonized over it. Many tears were shed at the feet of Jesus, where the truth became more important than life itself. Why the Lord continued working, teaching, forgiving, loving and training this sinner that I am, I do not know. Except... it is part of THE PLAN of God. YOU are part of THE PLAN, also. You know it. You feel it in your heart. If you don't "feel" it, go "do" it, and you will know it.

The "least of these" are not necessarily only the homeless. A person who was or is abused in any way (physically, sexually, emotionally, by neglect, etc.) can also be considered the "least of these." A person who has a roof above their head but not food in the house, or no electricity, or running water is considered one of the "least of these." A lonely widow or widower who is too old and poor to fix themselves healthy meals or get things done around the house like mowing the lawn, fixing a leaky roof or leaky plumbing or painting the house can be considered the "least of these."

Even the rich who are overwhelmed by the sudden loss of a loved one and are overcome with a spirit of mourning can be seen as the "least of these." That could be a ministry for you if you have been there.

"The Spirit of the Sovereign lord is on me, because the Lord has anointed me to...comfort all who mourn (afflicted, saddened), **and provide for those who grieve in Zion - to bestow on them a crown of beauty instead of ashes, the oil of gladness instead of mourning, and a garment of praise instead of a spirit of despair." (Isaiah 61:1-3)**

Drive around (or even better, walk) your neighborhood after you have prayed to the Lord that you may be able to see with the eyes of Jesus. Pray that the Lord put people in your way to whom you can minister. He will. And when He does, receive them with open arms and love.

There is a walking path at a park in my neighborhood. One day, when I started walking on that path, I asked the Lord to put somebody in my way to whom I could minister. After two minutes of walking, I crossed path with a man who looked sad and troubled. I asked him how he was doing, to which he unconvincingly replied, "OK." The Holy Spirit touched my heart that this was the man to whom I was supposed to minister.

This is what I suddenly told him, "Listen, I don't know you and you don't know me. So that makes me the best person for you to pour your heart out. Walk with me on this path and tell me your problem. I may never see you again, but know that whatever you tell me will not be shared with anyone. I will take everything you tell me to the Lord Jesus Christ in prayer."

The surprised man and I started walking together down the path, and he openly shared his spiritual and marital issues with me. The Holy Spirit immediately put in my heart the word to give to this man. I told him all that the Lord was wanting him to know. It was certainly a word of healing, as the man's countenance positively changed right away. Then we stopped, and I prayed for him right there and then. Only the Lord knew this man's heart and what he needed for healing.

As we walked back, we saw his wife coming up the path! We were about fifty feet away when the power of the Holy Spirit fell on her, and she began (with raised hands) to give thanks to Jesus and to worship the Lord. As we were all three together,

I repeated the message the Lord had for them. I then prayed for the both of them as they hugged each other. She had tears streaming down her cheeks as the Holy Spirit touched her heart. The man was visibly touched also, as he thought I was an angel sent by God to solve this "unsolvable" issue which was solved so quickly. I gave him my phone number in case he needed to talk further, and assured him that angels do not have phone numbers!

You will also have the "least of these" which you will see regularly; the poor, the hungry, the children, the homeless. They will seek you out, or you will go to them. You will get to know them and their special needs. God may give you just a handful or He may point out a greater need in your neighborhood circle. Pray to the Lord of the harvest that He may send you. I guarantee that you will rediscover you own neighborhood circle and see it in a way you never had before.

Some will come to your door with a special need, or to ask to mow your lawn or help out for extra cash. You may want to let them know sternly that they may not come to your door if they are intoxicated. You decide. Consider if you want to allow them to come into your home or not. Think it over carefully, understanding the consequences and then sticking by your policies so they may know where they stand.

After Jesus (who is our perfect example) was baptized, He ministered in His own neighborhood, also. Jesus started His ministry in His hometown of Nazareth, in Galilee.

"Jesus returned to Galilee in the power of the Spirit, and news about him spread through the whole countryside. He taught in their synagogues, and everyone praised him. He went to Nazareth, where he had been brought up..." (Luke 4:14-16)

Though Jesus started His ministry in His own neighborhood, He did not stay there long. He extended His ministry past His neighborhood and into the rest of Galilee. So must you extend your ministry beyond your neighborhood circle and into your town, city and county.

"Then he went down to Capernaum, a town in Galilee, and on the Sabbath began to teach the people." (Luke 4:31)

Part 3

The Outer Circle

"Go into all the world and preach the good news to all creation." (Mark 16:20)

"...and you will be my witnesses in Jerusalem, and in all Judea and Samaria, and to the ends of the earth." (Acts 1:8)

It was never meant for the gospel to stay safely in one place. Neither was it meant for you to stay within the safety of the walls of a church building. Nowhere in the Scriptures is Jesus recorded as saying, "Go, and be safe!" Going into the world requires us to get out of our comfort zone. Dare to go beyond the church walls! Yes, carry your cross.

The "church" is composed of those who believe in Christ Jesus and are saved (the bride of Christ), and does not necessarily mean that it is hemmed in by four walls. It is not about denomination or physical location. Church is not how large a building can be. Church is the people that are IN the building. You will not find anywhere in the Bible where the Lord said, "Go into the world and build bigger churches!" The bigger the church, the more pews you have for people to sit on. Yet, the Lord did say, "Go into all the world..."

The church does have a great purpose in teaching the gospel of Jesus Christ. With the organized funding of the church, thousands of missionaries have been able to bring millions to the salvation message of the gospel. Closer to home, churches have changed lives by serving communities with many programs for the old and young, with food pantries and clothes closets and many other programs. The church has been instrumental in teaching the gospel and discipling the saints of God. The church is the body of Christ, and you need to pray for the body of which you are a part. Though this revival will start in the street, many churches will eventually not only meet, but embrace the revival.

Church in America, however, has now become an overly comfortable sanctuary. You have a comfortable, padded place to sit, wonderful music every Sunday, temperature controlled environment, friends, a good sermon; everything organized for you. Just come in, sit down and receive. If Sunday morning is not enough, you may do it again on Sunday and Wednesday evenings when dinner might even be served! Certainly, a handful of saints do minister in the church as teachers, deacons, elders, administrators, etc.

However, one day you will get to heaven and the Lord will ask you what you did to serve Him. You will say, "I went to church every Sunday." Do you think that will impress the Lord? He will ask you, "Did you go into the world and make disciples?"

Saints of God, going out "into the world" is so much more important now as the end of the age approaches and Jesus returns for His church - His bride. Look at the fields, they are ripe for harvesting. Those fields are in your neighborhood and town! You who have been saved, it is time to rise up and "go" into the fields.

The biggest enemy of Christianity is not alcohol, drugs, homosexuality, godless government or schools - it's COMPLACENCY (self-satisfaction; smugness, being comfortable and wanting to stay just where you're at) on the part of Christians! It is now found perhaps more in the established church than it is in the streets!

The poor and homeless in the streets of your very own town or city are praying to God for someone like you to minister the love of Jesus Christ to them. You have grown in your neighborhood ministering experience, and it is now time to enlarge your field of harvest. You don't have far to go. You don't have to travel the world. The hungry in your city can use you and a thousand more like you. It is time to go and be a witness of what God has done for you.

That may be as simple as giving one hungry person some food; and then loving encouragement; and then the testimony of Jesus Christ; and then prayer. You are the harvester of that ripe, golden wheat in your field. Pluck that poor man's soul from the lowly street and bring it up to the grain storage bin of heaven. If you don't, and the harvest rots in the field, what will you tell the Lord when you finally come before Him?

Don't fear, don't be afraid to "go." You can make a difference one homeless person at a time. Do not be overwhelmed with the great need in the street. Jesus said in **Matthew 25:40, "...whatever you did for ONE of the least of these...you did for me."** Jesus did not say, "...for a thousand of the least of these!" You may be the one to end up ministering to a thousand...but it starts with one at a time.

When you come before the Lord, He will ask you what you did. You will answer, "I took care of one of the 'least of these' every week and brought food and clothing, encouragement and prayer." The Lord will be pleased that you were trustworthy with one of the "least of these," according to His Word. You did "go" beyond the walls of the church and into the street.

Yes, there are many more who need ministering in the street. Not just homeless men, women and children, but also those who are just twenty-four hours from being homeless. You may not be able to help them all; simply help the needy, one at a time, according to the gifts God has so graciously given you - God's grace through you.

I just found out last week about a ninety-two year old woman in my town who makes homemade quilts and gives them to homeless men and women who live in a camp, under a tent or other "secure" place. The homeless man living under a bridge, who was the recipient of her beautiful quilt, spoke of her in awe, as if God himself had given it to him. This man knew he was loved. The quilt came with love and prayers for this homeless man.

It took a while for that older saint of God to make that quilt. She could have sold it for a tidy sum. However, being able to make these quilts is her gift from God, her ministry to the least of these. The Holy Spirit guides her as to who should receive her anointed quilts. She has **pity** (filled with compassion) on the poor and is **gracious** (able to give undeserved but freely given love and favor) to the homeless...one at a time.

(Please note that these words in parenthesis - **pity, gracious, mercy** - are very important. Review and memorize their meaning. Your ministry cannot grow in Holy Spirit power without these words being actively present in your relationship with the "least of these.")

Truly, your ministry may be as simple as having **mercy** (compassion, kindness, forgiveness) on the "least of these" and making sure they are first fed. What you feed them is up to you. Bean burritos were suggested. However, you can make sandwiches or simple hot meals. Your imagination (and your heart) is the limit. Don't fix them anything you would not eat yourself! Other than lovingly ministering the gospel of Jesus Christ, food should be the first and most important physical ministry to the least of these.

"Which of these three (the priest, the Levite, a Samaritan) **do you think was a neighbor to the man who fell into the hands of robbers?" The expert in the law replied, 'The one who had mercy on him.' Jesus told him, 'Go and do likewise.'" (Luke 10:36, 37)**

Part 4

Where's The Money?

Though your imagination and your heart have a big impact on what you physically provide for the poor, your pocketbook is nevertheless of utmost importance. Though you could personally supply the homeless with all their needs (food, clothing, other basic necessities), you will not have all those ministries yourself. You may provide food, someone else some clothing, and another person may supply basic needs.

For example: If there are three of you, one can bring a main food item (burrito, sandwich); another can bring sweets and drinks; and another clothing. If there are two of you, split it up as to what you can afford. If there is only one of you, find someone else to help you!

On any given day, I like to buy a couple bags of bean burritos to give out to the homeless. I have a good brother in Christ, Bill Weaver, who comes with me and brings the homeless their beloved apple and cherry pies, and water. Brother Bill has been consistent in visiting the homeless. He has a heart for the homeless and loves them dearly. They love him and affectionately call him the "Pie Man!" He could also be called the prayer man, the fellowship man, the glove man, the battery man, the drinks man... etc. From time to time, his precious wife, Glenda, comes with him to minister and love these special children of God, the "least of these" in the street. Glory to God!

You should spend a personal minimum of twenty-five dollars a week on your ministry to the "least of these."

Having said that, I understand that this may be a lot for some people. You may only have ten dollars available. Rejoice, you can buy ten pairs of white socks for eight dollars (Walmart). Some of you may be able to afford fifty, a hundred, and for some two hundred dollars a week may not be much! Now that you have a ministry, how much are you willing to invest in it? Know that whatever you spend on the poor will result in you being blessed abundantly.

"Give, and it will be given to you. A good measure, pressed down, shaken together and running over, will be poured into your lap. For with the measure you use, it will be measured to you." (Luke 6:38)

I understand you have to live and pay your bills, and put a little aside for rainy days. Strangely enough, I have never seen saints of God (including myself) who give "as unto the Lord," and are not blessed with more than enough for their own needs. Of course, one must use wisdom, but there is something supernatural about giving for God's purpose.

If you have twelve people in your home meeting group and you each give twenty-five dollars a week, that pumps three hundred dollars into your town's homeless economy per week (per home meeting group). Let's say we are successful in spreading God's plan for the ministry to the "least of these." Within a certain amount of time we have 4,000 such home meeting groups throughout the United States (that is not really a high number and this is applicable anywhere in the world, though the amount of money will be different). Suddenly, you find that 4,000 times three hundred dollars equals 1.2 million dollars for the homeless! And that's a minimum. My prayer is that before I go on to be with the Lord, I would like to see at least 100,000 such home meetings in these U. S. of A.

You might say, "That amount doesn't take care of all the homeless." One at a time, saints of God, one at a time. Remember, your first priority is their spiritual welfare.

You are actually able to spend much more than that. Why? Because you take donations. People will hear about what you are doing and unsolicited donations will start trickling in. If you are not shy about telling others about your ministry and letting them know that you take donations, you will receive more. You will also receive donations of clothing, shoes, and anything else the homeless can use.

There is no need to form a non-profit organization. There is no need for tax filing unless the financial gifts you receive are over the maximum gift one can receive under U.S. IRS and your state laws. However, you should keep your own record of donations received. The people giving to you will get their blessing from the Lord, but you want your blessing, also. So, do give of your own, also!

"Araunah said to David, 'Let my lord the king take whatever pleases him and offer it up.'...But the king replied to Araunah, 'No, I insist on paying you for it. I will not sacrifice to the Lord my God burnt offerings that cost me nothing.'" (2 Samuel 24:22, 24)

ONE HUNDRED PERCENT OF ALL DONATIONS YOU COLLECT FOR YOUR MINISTRY MUST GO TO THE POOR AND HOMELESS. THIS IS NOT YOUR MONEY.

You are accountable to God. Do not spend money given for the poor by spending even just one penny of it on yourself. Do not lose God's blessing because of such an abomination. Receive donations, honor the Lord and glorify His Holy Name.

If you have an issue with money, get back in your "little circle" and have a little talk with "Daddy." Bring the subject up at a home meeting and let others impart their wisdom upon you. Let prayers go up for you at the home meeting circle. Be open about this issue, though I strongly suspect others may already know if you have a need for better money management.

If you are vocal about your ministry, you will also receive clothing, shoes, etc., from your friends, family, church members and other saints of God. You may receive a coat, shirt, jeans or pair of shoes that you really "covet" (want for yourself). Listen to me, saints of God; give it to the poor! Do not keep it and use it for yourself! It was given for the poor and should go directly to the poor.

However, if you go to a thrift store and buy an armful of clothing for those in need, this is a different situation if you have spent your OWN money. You may later on decide to keep a shirt or pair of jeans you have "coveted." That is all right. It's your own money, not money given to you as a donation for the poor. Likewise, it's not clothing that was given to you as a donation for the homeless.

The minimum $25.00 you contribute is to be used directly for the physical needs of the poor and homeless. Do not start deducting your gas expense, lunch, personal needs on the day you minister, etc. That comes out of your own pocket. Twenty-five dollars (or whatever amount you set) should go wholly, completely, 100% to the "least of these." However, use wisdom and spend all that you are able on the "least of these."

You might also look around your home to see what can be used for the homeless. In fact, give some of your clothes away that have been hanging for so long in the closet (or the garage, attic, basement or storage shed). Don't kid yourself, you're not ever going to wear those again! How much clothing do you need anyhow, when there are some in the street who have but one set? How many pairs of shoes does a person need? Give, saints of God, give.

"'...every tree that does not produce good fruit will be cut down and thrown into the fire.'

'What should we do then?' the crowd asked. John answered, 'The man with two tunics (a garment reaching to the knees and worn without a belt) **should share with him who has none, and the one who has food should do the same.'" (Luke 3:9-11)**

CHAPTER *thirteen*

Go!

Part 1

Decentralization

You have seen that in THE PLAN God has for you to minister to the homeless you have a little circle (you), an expanded circle (home meetings), a larger circle (your neighborhood) and an outer circle (your city). All these circles work together (like a bicycle wheel) to move your ministry forward and make you a spark in the streets, eventually lighting on fire a ground roots revival in your city.

If you provide the spark, God will provide the fire!

You now understand that home meetings are an integral part of this plan. You have by now enjoyed life-transforming testimonies, and training and prayer time with other saints of God who are called as you are. You have found out that you are not forming yet another church, but instead are building a solid ministry to the "least of these" from the bottom up, according to God's plan.

Home meetings do away with all the expenses that bog down the church establishment. Of all the churches I have visited in my hometown, NONE budgeted over TWO percent of the total church budget for the poor. You, however, do not have to pay a church mortgage, salaries, upkeep, maintenance, utilities, administration, etc. You do not form an organization - non-profit or otherwise - with all the legal expenses, reports, and headaches. You can spend all your time and resources (100%) serving, honoring and glorifying the Lord by taking care of His special children, the "least of these."

Simple is good.

We do not at all advocate doing away with or shunning the established church! The church is, in fact, much needed for maintaining doctrinal integrity. Having home meetings does not mean that you should neglect to attend your church meetings, especially on Sunday when you touch bases and fellowship with your church family.

Yes, established churches may disagree on some points of the scriptures. However, bible believing churches who believe on Jesus Christ as the resurrected Son of the Living God; and believe in salvation not by works but by grace, have much to offer if you have questions about biblical doctrine. Every ship that sails stormy waters needs a safe port to which he can return.

However, no matter what doctrinal answers you get or where you get them from, make sure you take it to the Lord in prayer for confirmation. It must be confirmed through the Bible, the Word of God. Be patient and wait for confirmation before you act on a questionable doctrinal interpretation. As we learned in the section on home meetings, Jesus is in charge.

You also learned that your ministry must expand into your city. It is initially as simple as going in town, finding a homeless person, feeding him (her), talking with him, respecting his human, personal and spiritual dignity (whether he is drunk or not), and loving him in the name of Jesus. Now, go to the next one...and the next...and the next, etc.; one at a time. You may have to minister to some of them for a year before they trust you and allow you to minister Jesus to them. Consistency on your part is of essence (a necessity).

You may have seen by now how part of God's plan works. By having a neighborhood ministry, a group at home meetings, and a wider number of saints of God in the city, you have formed a network of "emergency" responders. You have the connections, the trained people, the resources, the knowledge to act when there suddenly comes a great need. That need may be due to a hurricane, a bad storm or flood, a blizzard or a tornado.

However, the greatest need will most likely be of a spiritual nature. Prayer may be immediately needed for an imminent calamity or a great personal need. The call can immediately go through the ministry so as to cancel the enemy's advances and bring victory in the name of Jesus Christ. The critical need may be a miraculous healing, protection or the comforting of a neighborhood or city. Whenever prayer is needed, your network of responders is available.

Will the homeless help in an emergency or pray when you need them to? Absolutely! I have heard powerful and also very sweet prayers coming from the "least of these." What an all- inclusive and perfect plan God has for us!

You have also learned that while the church is centralized, your ministry is decentralized. Normally, the "least of these" must go to the church, the "center," to get help. Everyone in need must come to the church to get benefits; that is centralized help.

In "decentralized" help, you go out of the church and into the street to help the "least of these." You meet them where they are, at their level. You go to them because many of them cannot or will not go into a church (not to mention, Jesus said, "Go").

The difference between your ministry and the established church is that your ministry is out of confining walls and into the street where the revival will begin. Your ministry reflects more accurately the first century church which was operating under persecution. They had no choice but to go into the street. You have learned to dare to go beyond the church. God has good reasons for that. He knows the future and He is preparing you now.

You've also learned where the money is - it's in your wallet! You must now take it out of your wallet and make an investment in your ministry. Your investment is not just in time, blood, sweat and tears, but in money. That money is part of your sacrifice, part of you dying on the cross. I know it's hard, but let it go! Carry your cross. Strange how the saints of God are willing to give everything and do all, until it comes to their money. That's not your money, anyhow. It's God's all along. Remember, the Lord gives, and the Lord takes away. So don't be stingy and do not hold back. Give generously and directly to your ministry and help your unbelief by seeing God bless you supernaturally in return.

"'If you can?'" said Jesus. "Everything is possible for him who believes."

Immediately the boy's father exclaimed, "I do believe; help me overcome my unbelief!" (Mark 9:23, 24)

Part 2

Your Ministry

This list of ministries to help the "least of these" will be incomplete. Only your imagination and the leading of the Holy Spirit will complete it. I would love to hear from you to hear of new ministries that I have not heard or thought of before. I have found by experience the ministries that are truly needed. To find a ministry to the homeless, FIND THEIR NEED. It's not about you - what you would want. Think about THEM.

To find their need, you must get up close and pay attention. You must empathize (as if you yourself are suffering) with their situation. It's sympathy which says, "Oh, I feel bad for you." But empathy says, "If you hurt, I hurt." Not being saved is the biggest "hurt." Ministering the gospel of Jesus Christ is the primary and ongoing ministry.

I had a homeless man tell me he had problems with rats at night. The rats would walk across his face while he was sleeping, and wake him up. The previous night, he was sleeping very soundly when he felt something tugging at his left hand, which was out of his sleeping bag. Half asleep, he turned to look and saw a rat aggressively gnawing at his little finger. He immediately woke up and shook the rat off his bloody finger to let the rat know he wasn't dead. The next day, this man showed me an open sore where part of the palm side of his little finger had been eaten! That day I brought him two rat traps. That night he caught three rats and has had no problems since with rats eating his extremities!

If you, yourself, hurt while reading this true story, then you empathized - if he hurt, you hurt. My knowing his need made his life much more comfortable. The whole $1.95 I spent on the traps probably also helped prevent the bubonic plague in my city!

We are not looking to start "big" projects, here. Big projects mean you are centralizing, again. You may want to have a place where the homeless can be fed or a place for them to sleep. Immediately, you are putting four walls around your ministry. If someone needs help with alcoholism, or mental/emotional issues, or drug abuse, or some other issue which needs permanent locations for counseling and guidance, look to already existing programs. Know where these programs are available in your town and take the poor there. You may be the one with the gift of organization to start something big, but just make sure it is the Lord who is guiding you. Make sure you are abiding by THE PLAN of the Lord.

You may be active in one or more of the following ministries. As the seasons change, so may your ministries. The "winter coats" ministry will not be popular in the summer! Find something else to do. Remember, the homeless will not take more with them than they can carry on their back.

1. Food Ministry

Some of you "mother earth" types will want to make sure the homeless eat only what is good for them! You want to bring them whole wheat this, and Vitamin D that, low fat goodies and low carbohydrate snacks. Certainly, sliced white bread is out (yuck and yuck)! However, they are used to going behind the doughnut store after hours and picking up boxes and boxes of doughnuts for dinner (and breakfast, and lunch).

I once asked a homeless man if he wanted a flashlight. His eyes got big and he got really excited. "Yes, I sure do!" he exclaimed. After I had given him the small flashlight, he thanked me profusely and gave me a big hug. I asked him why he was so excited about a flashlight. He said, "Because now I'll be able to see what I'm eating when I go dumpster diving!"

You can prepare sandwiches yourself (whole wheat bread, of course) - ham and cheese (throw some lettuce on that, please, tomato on the side, mayo, mustard, ketchup), peanut butter and jelly, or whatever is tasty and keeps when it's hot outside. Prepared hot dogs don't work because they shrivel up and taste like cardboard as they cool (and they cool fast). Whatever you fix, make it as tasty as you can - the way you would like it. Make it a treat for them.

My favorite is the humble bean burrito - protein rich, good tasting, sticks to your ribs, keeps well, easy to handle, stays warm, cheap, with a variety of taco sauces available. I get them at Taco Bell. Your area (or country) may have something similar. Empathize!

Whatever you bring, be consistent. Be known for what you bring, and they will look forward to you coming with that particular food. However, remain open to improvement and do ask if they are tired of what you are bringing them. Is there something better you could bring? Most often they will not say anything until you ask.

They will ask you why you're doing this for them. That's when you tell them about the love of Jesus. Remember, their spiritual welfare is of first importance. However, just don't push preaching down their throat. Do let them know, "If Jesus loves you, I love you."

The homeless sure love their carbohydrates! Bring lots of apple or cherry pies (the small individually wrapped kind), moon pies, cinnamon rolls, chocolate anything, individual cakes, and anything else sweet. You can go to Day-Old Bakeries and get some good deals.

To wash all that food down, you can get them individual water bottles (16 or 20 oz.). If you get them Pepsi in a can, do NOT get the diet kind. Again, they want all the carbs they can get. They love their sodas! They also love Yahoos (chocolate milk drink).

So, one person can get food, and another can bring the drinks and snacks. If you bring drinks, please bring them in an ice box - with ice. Would you want a warm soda or bottle of water during the summer? I have known some saints of God who drove around and brought hot coffee or hot chocolate to the homeless in the street during the Holidays, when it's cold.

Prepare the food, drinks and snacks so they are easy to give away. Don't fix sandwiches after you get to the homeless. Have the foods prepared and ready to go before you get there. This way, you can keep on moving and see as many homeless as possible in your allotted time. Once, or maybe twice a week is good. Maybe Wednesdays and Sundays. Go over the best times to visit with those that are in camps.

You may be able to bring food that someone in camp can heat up. You can provide some camps with a one-burner gas camping stove. Then you will have to provide them with a small canister of propane gas per week. They will tell you what they like or need, though Ramen Noodles is always a winner. Always be honest with the "least of these" and ask them what you can do for them if you aren't sure. Many of the homeless get food stamps, though it may be minimal. Everything helps. If they don't get food stamps, help them sign up.

You'll be surprised at what they ask for, sometimes. We had one man who's most important need was a leaf rake! He wanted to keep his camp clean. Brother Dennis McReynolds bought him a used one he found for five dollars. The homeless man was camping near a park, and in fact kept the whole park raked clean! Everyone walking by remarked how immaculately raked was this particular park. He was very happy with his rake, as it made him feel more fulfilled and useful to society!

2. Clothing Ministry

When it's hot in the summertime, shorts and T-shirts are in order. Wintertime is a little bit more involved. They will need coats, fleeces, sweaters, sweatshirts, long pants, long underwear, gloves and hats. Ponchos, which take very little space, are great any time of the year.

Do not give the homeless any white clothing! They do not stay white long.

You may want to find out where the church clothes closets are and bring the homeless there. It's better for you to spend time and gas to get them there rather than spend money on buying them clothes, especially during the winter.

Alternatively, you can go to thrift shops, second hand stores, Goodwill and rescue mission stores to find good deals on clothes. You can stop at garage sales where you can sometimes find jeans and shoes at a great price. Or/and, you can solicit clothing from everyone you know, including family, friends, neighbors, church family, etc. Proclaim your ministry to everyone (notice I did not say "brag about").

All dry-cleaners have unclaimed clothes stored somewhere in their back room. Sometimes they sell the lot. But if you tell them it will be for the homeless, they may just give you a stack of free clothing! Even if you have to pay a little, it would be a great deal.

3. Sock Ministry

Socks are worth their weight in gold in the street. The homeless are not always able to do laundry. They wear their white socks until they turn brown and fall off their feet, at which point they uncomfortably wear their shoes without socks. Though white socks are the standard, you may want to carry some grey or black ones, also. Wool socks for the winter would be awesome, though they are more expensive. White socks can be had for 75-85 cents each (Walmart).

4. Shoe Ministry

A new pair of shoes (tennis shoes being most popular) can get the homeless really excited. Blessing them with a pair of shoes is an important moment. Again, thrift stores and garage sales are a good source. You may visit all the shoe stores in your town and see if they will contribute shoes to your ministry.

There is a twelve-year old young man from Cranston, Rhode Island, with a loving and giving heart who has so far donated more than 10,000 pairs of shoes to needy children! He solicited shoe stores to donate all the shoes. Nicholas Lowinger (with mom and dad's help) formed the Gotta Have Sole Foundation, www.gottahavesole.org (CNN, September 22, 2013).

Other than shoes, you can get them boots for the winter, and flip-flops in the summer. When you get flip-flops, don't get the little flimsy ones with the skinny, plastic thong between the toes. Get as good quality as you are willing to afford. It is better to get six good pairs to give away rather than fifty bad pairs to throw away.

5. Bibles Ministry

The whole Bible or just a New Testament would be awesome. Make that large print, and you've got a winner. Many churches will give out Bibles. But if the homeless do not have one, make sure you have some on hand. This is at the heart of the homeless ministry.

6. Reading Glasses Ministry

The best thing I have given to a man was a pair of reading glasses. He now could read the New Testament a lady had given him. He was extremely overjoyed and would quote me new scripture he had memorized every time I saw him.

A man's thumb got seriously infected when he could not pull out the splinter in his thumb because he could not see it. Reading glasses helped him.

Your can get good, clear reading glasses at Walmart for about $2.75 a pair (in quantity). That is a cheap price for a man to be able to read the Word of God! You should carry mostly 2.00 glasses, though you should also have some pairs of 1.50 and 2.50 glasses.

You can find some pairs at discount stores that may cost you just one dollar each. DON'T buy them! Clear sight is important. Go for the best quality you can afford.

7. Pets of the Homeless Ministry

Some of the homeless have dogs which need flea treatment, rabies shots, heart worm medicine, food, collars, leashes, shampoo, brushes, etc. You can provide some of these things, and you can also find out which vet in your town will do the rest for free. You can drive the owner and pet to the vet and get that done. The homeless love their pets and usually take good care of them. A dog is a very important, comforting, loyal companion for the "least of these," and brings a little healing into their lives.

8. Radio, Batteries Ministry

A radio keeps the homeless in touch with what is happening in the rest of the world. Plus, they can listen to a football or baseball game, the news or the weather once in a while. Communication with the world makes them feel less isolated and less likely to be depressed. A radio is very important as a source of entertainment. You can get little transistor radios for a few dollars. Wind-up radios are not liked too well, so batteries are in order.

9. Bicycle Ministry

For the poor or homeless, a bicycle is a big ticket item which makes life a lot easier for those who work, but have no vehicle. Make sure you know that a particular person actually needs a bike and will keep it. The reason I say this is because many of the homeless will take a bike, which is often too willingly given, then sell it the next day for extra cash. That cash may very well go to buying beer. We don't want to go there.

If you are gifted mechanically, you can buy cheap second hand bikes, fix them, and thus provide transportation to someone in need. Then pray over the bike for the safety of the user. So many of the homeless get hurt riding their bikes while intoxicated - some seriously. Counsel them on that subject before you give them a bike.

Also, make sure that a secure lock comes with every bike for obvious reasons. Theft of bikes is common amongst street people. If you see the recipient of your bike a week later, and he doesn't have a bike anymore, that's life. Let it go. Don't get on his case. It might have been stolen or sold. It doesn't matter because now some other homeless person is using that bike. You have a ministry to the homeless, right? And the homeless are using your bikes, right? Why should you complain? Let the dust fall where it will! Glory to God!

10. Tents, Sleeping Bags, Blankets, Tarps Ministry

Obviously, you can't do all of these; pick one or two. Make sure you don't get a real bulky blanket which is hard to pack and carry around. It's a different story if they have a base camp. Tarps are used to cover the tents to protect them from the rain. They can also use the tarps to make a lean-to. Sleeping bags need to be light, with synthetic insulation. Down sleeping bags are great, but expensive and useless if wet. They will get wet.

11. Bus Pass Ministry

You can buy these cards at the city or county bus office. They are good for seven to ten rides, or so. Give only one at a time. Any extras that you give away could be too easily sold. Don't just hand them out to all, but only to those who work or have doctor or other appointments to go to.

12. Backpack Ministry

You can buy them new or used whenever you see one at garage sales. If you buy them new, tear the tags off so they can't return them to the store for cash in order to buy...beer. Almost all of the homeless need a backpack.

13. Fishing Pole and Fishing Gear Ministry

If you live by the sea or a large lake, the homeless will catch fish to eat or sell (mostly to sell). No need to buy new. Like bikes, fishing poles come...and go. If they are making an income with their fishing pole, they will make sure to keep an eye on it so it doesn't get stolen. Neither will they sell it. Don't ever ask them what they did with whatever you gave them. Give as unto the Lord and let it go.

14. Personal Hygiene Kits Ministry

You should not put all needed items for normal good hygiene in one bag to be handed out. You should carry all these items separately and hand out only what they need.

I was once ministering to a group of homeless men when I asked them if they wanted some toothpaste and a toothbrush. They all looked at me with a puzzled look, and all started smiling at the same time. Then they burst into laughter! As they did, I could see that some had no teeth, some just a few, some had loose front teeth and otherwise such poor dental health that a toothbrush had by now become irrelevant. I put the toothbrush and toothpaste away.

These items (in order of importance) are needed; disinfectant wipes (personal package size), nail clippers, toilet paper (for camps), shavers and cream, soap, shampoo, comb. Small sample sizes are handy.

15. First Aid/Medical Ministry

They could probably all use a handful of Band-Aids and a small tube of antibiotic cream. Most don't care about or treat cuts, gashes, bruises, etc., which most often happens when falling while riding a bike under the influence. This is a good time for prayer! They will gladly accept prayer for healing of their battered bodies.

I once met a homeless man named Jack, whose hand was swollen three times its size due to an infected cut. He was using a profuse amount of hydrogen peroxide someone had given him, which was rotting his hand away. He was getting sick, and I was afraid the spreading infection would kill him. He did not want to see a doctor. His wife had died of a heart attack while with him in the street a couple of weeks before, and he was a little despondent. I told him he needed to soak his hand in hot salt water three or four times a day for twenty minutes each time. Since he was in a camp, I got him a little one burner gas stove and an aluminum pan. As we sat on the ground, I showed him how to heat the water, add the salt and soak his hand.

I came twice a day to make sure he did it right and to show him how to bandage his hand the right way. I supplied him with bandages and antibiotic cream. After a few days, we started making headway and his hand slowly started to heal.

After two or three weeks of treatment, his hand was starting to get back to normal. Of course, I prayed for his healing every time I saw him and while at home.

I saw Jack in the street a few months later all healed up and doing great. He came up to me and said, "You saved my life!" I told him that the Lord saved his life after we prayed for him. He replied, "A lot of people prayed for me. You took care of me. Nobody has taken care of me like that before." This tough, bearded, weathered homeless man began to weep openly... and we hugged.

Do you understand what kind of medical treatment and healing is needed in the street?

16. Identification Cards/Birth Certificates Ministry

These documents are so very important in our society. Without them the homeless cannot get benefits due them; disability benefits, food stamps, job, a stay at some homeless shelters, travel. No matter what state they're from, birth certificate duplicates are readily available online. Also, lost or stolen licenses can often be replaced by a simple visit to the Department of Motor Vehicles with proof of identification (birth certificate) and a small fee.

A saint of God with administrative gifting can easily help the homeless with the issue of missing identification. However, check in your town, as some churches or organizations offer that service for the homeless. If someone else can do it, it's just a matter of explaining the process to those in need and driving them to the location.

17. Homeless Survival Guide Ministry

This is a low cost, little pamphlet which can be researched and put together listing all the services available to the poor and homeless. It can contain valuable information about abuse hotline, animal control, blind services, child care, medical/dental care, disability help, eye glasses, financial assistance, food stamps, veterans' assistance, shelters, transportation, and a host of other relevant listings. Each listing could list the address, phone number and a short synopsis of help available, days and times open.

These pamphlets (I'm now holding one four by eight inches, with thirty pages) can be passed out to all the churches and organizations that cater to the "least of these" so that all those in need may be handed one. You may get sponsors who can help pay for the expense of printing.

18. Solar Showers Ministries

Aaaah! A nice hot shower is so therapeutic. The homeless can step in a hot shower if you provide them with solar hot showers. It is simply a dark colored plastic bag with a little hose and a small shower head which can be hung from a tree. You fill it up with water and leave it in the sun for a couple of hours and voilà, hot water. They are available at camping supply stores for twelve to twenty dollars. This item would be a pleasant addition to any homeless camp.

20. Hair Cutting Ministry

Going to a barber or buying electric shears are too expensive for the "least of these." You would not even have to know how to cut hair, as most of the homeless simply have their hair sheared off. You can get battery operated shears. You may also get regular electric shears, run a small inverter (25 watts would be enough, as the shears I have are 12 watts) hooked up to a car battery and shear away. You may be able to find 12 v. shears to plug in your car cigarette lighter. Either way, you would be in big demand and greatly appreciated. If you could really cut hair you could cut the ladies' hair, too.

21. Holding Services

Holding services by itself will not bring the homeless to attend. Food must be included. You can hold services outdoors, under a park pavilion or picnic shelter, under a small canopy tent, or anywhere where you can get some shelter. In dry climates, it can simply be in the open.

Talk it over with the poor or homeless to whom you minister. Say, "Hey, I'm thinking of fixing y'all a big spaghetti dinner the last Sunday of the month. We'll have a little word from the bible first, and then we'll have a freshly cooked spaghetti dinner (describe it). What do you say?" For the first two or three meetings, mention it three to four weeks ahead of time, every time you see them. If you are consistent, you might not see some for a month, but they will be there the last Sunday of the month.

They will come to see what you have. If you preach "fire and brimstone," you won't see them again. If you preach/teach the love of God, forgiveness and repentance, you'll have a crowd. Don't preach more than FIFTEEN MINUTES, or you will lose them. Don't advertise all over town, or you'll have two hundred people before you know it! First invite those to whom you minister regularly and want at your meeting. If they like what you are doing, they will invite others. As they are mainly sober and somewhat respectful of Sundays, you will see them at their best.

An affordable dinner is a spaghetti dinner with meatballs (real meat, not soy balls), sauce, fresh French bread (thickly sliced), parmesan cheese, a sweet desert, Pepsi and water. Get a couple of gas burners, pots, etc., and cook it fresh right there and then. A spaghetti dinner is great because you can fix enough based on who comes to the service. There is no guessing and no leftovers to take home or throw away.

Music is great. If you can have someone play the guitar, sing the old hymns. Many of the homeless remember the old hymns from their days of their youth in church; and they will love to sing along. It's amazing how they remember all the words to the songs.

If anybody asks you what you are doing, you are having a family reunion! You can feed thirty people for about three dollars and fifty cents each. Split it up among three or four people and it's not that bad. If it comes down to it, you can do it by yourself.

If you have more than fifty people, your group may become too noticeable, and a permit may then be required of you. You may then have to find a large room in a building somewhere for the last Sunday of the month.

The best time for a service is the LAST Sunday of the month. By that time, the disability or social security check received on the first of the month has been spent, and they are now hungry. You could probably also hold a service on the third Sunday, but the first or second Sunday will get you very few takers. Starting the service at eleven or twelve noon is good. Hold the service first, then eat! They are usually gone within an hour after finishing eating.

Pat is a dear sister in the Lord who emailed me once and compassionately asked me why I was not bringing the "least of these" to our church. Not only does she remember our ministry in her prayers, but Pat is an amazing worshipper of the Lord our God, and an encourager when I need it most. She is full of the love of the Lord, a true saint of God. She keeps our ministry in mind and has often contributed to our ministry with clothing, shoes and other items. Many people will ask you the same question Pat asked, which is why I am including my emailed response.

I go in the street to minister to them because the Lord said "Go..." The center of the world is not in the "church establishment," but where the unsaved are - in the street. When we go in the street, we are the church. When I hold a service in the street, the homeless and the poor rejoice that they have had "church." We have music, we worship, I preach the Word of God, and we all glorify the Holy name of Jesus as the family of God.

They can freely come as they are, whether they've had a beer or not, with clean or dirty clothes, smelly or unshaven, whether they walk or ride a bike, on time or late, without being judged or condemned.

Then I fix and feed them all a full, wholesome meal which we all eat together. Do I have any help? Yes, the homeless help me off-load my truck, set everything up, serve the food, cleanup, pack everything back up, etc. We all work together. I never have to ask for help.

Sometimes there are children of the poor, and sometimes a dog or two. We fellowship, we laugh, and maybe shed a tear or two as we pray for some of them. We have unity and we love one another. On that day, they are reminded they are loved. When it's all said and done, I fed and loved Jesus himself.

It's real - no games, no politics. It's scriptural. It's the only day they truly feel like a family.

And you want me to bring them to our "church?"

22. Bug Ministry

Obviously, there is a need for a way to kill the flies, mosquitoes, cockroaches, rats and mice where the homeless live. As I have stated previously, mice and rat traps go a long way to making life more comfortable and safe for the homeless.

Mosquitoes, biting flies, and gnats are a hindrance and can be taken care of by giving the homeless a can of personal bug spray every now and then (20% DEET, minimum). I have sat with them long enough to truly appreciate the relief such ministry brings! There are other available bug products you could bring, maybe in addition to your other ministry (ies).

The further south you go the bigger the cockroaches are. I believe they reach their biggest by the time you get to Florida! Having cockroaches crawl over your neck, face, lips, nose and inside your ears while you are sleeping will hinder your sleep, not to mention your health (do you empathize yet?). If the area is protected from the weather or is relatively dry, Boric Acid powder works best and is most economical. You can also use a variety of roach traps.

The next biggest issue in a somewhat permanent camp is rats and mice. Poison should not be used, as other animals (especially cats) may be killed. Use the old fashion traps which are economical and effective. You may need to supply them with a jar of peanut butter for bait.

23. Firewood Ministry

As the homeless would rather have fires that don't smoke, dry oak firewood would be ideal. Firewood cut up in small pieces is supplied to two of our camps during the winter. They use it for heating and cooking.

I had a ministry in the Blue Ridge Mountains a few years ago. There were (and still are) some people living in houses with no electricity or gas. They drew their water out of a well with a hand pump, and cooked and heated with wood. Some of them were too old to cut enough wood for the winter and too poor to buy some. I cut and split some firewood myself, and also took donations of firewood from our congregation.

There was this one old, little, pioneering widow who lived way out in the woods and hardly ever had a visitor. She wouldn't make the journey to church anymore, so on Sunday afternoons I would go and bring church to her, and I would share the love of

Jesus Christ with her. She looked forward to my bringing my wife and children and visiting with her for a couple of hours a week.

She grew a garden, put away food for the winter, and raised some chickens and some turkeys. Whenever I brought her some firewood cut just the right size for her cooking stove, she never failed to make sure I left with fresh apples, or potatoes, a batch of greens, a mess of dry beans, or canned goodies and sometimes even a chicken or a turkey to take home with us for dinner. They weren't always dead and plucked, either!

25. Tent City

If you have the gift of organization and administration, not to mention fundraising, you may be able to establish a "tent city" for the homeless. You'll need a plot of land OUTSIDE THE CITY LIMITS to organize tents and facilities in an orderly fashion. Some cities are doing this. There are communities, such as Dignity Village in Portland Oregon, which has been there since the year 2000. "The 'ecovillage' set up by homeless people is hygienic and self-sufficient." (What Tent Cities Say About America, Arjun Sethi, www.cnn.com/2013/12/23/opinion/sethi-tent-cities/index. html?hpt=hp_bn7)

I know it's a big, centralized project, but it is really needed.

26. Homeless Learning Center

I'm going to let your imagination run with this one!

27. Adopt-a-Homeless/Poor Family

It is done all over the world. Isn't it time you establish it in your hometown?

28. Librarian Ministry

That's right, many of the homeless like to read! Bring them books of the genres they enjoy; westerns, thrillers, war, etc. Or how about getting books to children in need?

29. Day Labor Breakfast Ministry

If you are an early bird, this ministry could be for you. Men will meet at a day labor office starting at 5:00 in the morning hoping to snag a job for the day. Many of these poor/homeless men are looking for work on an empty stomach. Wouldn't it be nice if someone had some breakfast sandwiches and a drink ready for them before they go off to work? Or maybe, you could fix a bag lunch they could take with them. Or both! If they can't get a job that day, at least they have eaten.

Internet sites that you may want to look at:
streetandlanesministry.com (decentralized homeless ministry)
pensacolahomeless.com (see an example of a "Survival Guide", and other homeless ministries)
agrm.org (Association of Gospel Rescue Missions)
hud.gov/homeless, nmha.org or **mentalhealthamerica.net** (if you really need to know)
lazarusatl.org (good decentralized ministry to the homeless in Atlanta, Georgia)

"Is not this the kind of fasting I have chosen: to loose the chains of injustice and untie the cords of the yoke, to set the oppressed free and break every yoke? Is it not to share your food with the hungry and to provide the poor wanderer with shelter - when you see the naked, to clothe him, and not turn away from your own flesh and blood?

Then your light will break forth like the dawn, and your healing will quickly appear; then your righteousness will go before you, and the glory of the Lord will be your rear guard.

Then you will call, and the Lord will answer; you will cry for help, and he will say: Here am I." (Isaiah 58:6-9)

CHAPTER *fourteen*

Just Do It

Part 1

Stand Tall And See Well

Most of what follows is common sense. Nevertheless, I have written it down for those who have doubts about one issue or another concerning the ministry to the "least of these." You must allow yourself to being led of the Holy Spirit rather than simply abiding by a bunch of rules (the law). That's why individual prayer (your little circle) and corporate prayer (your home meeting circle) are so important. Come at the feet of Jesus and learn to hear His voice and have Him guide you.

You all have different personalities and you may all tackle problems and issues differently. However, this you must all have in common; love deeply and respect the dignity of the "least of these."

"Now that you have purified yourselves by obeying the truth so that you have sincere love for your brothers, love one another deeply, from the heart." (1 Peter 1:22)

The "least of these" don't care if you have failed high school algebra or if you even have a college degree or if you've been married once or twice or if you took drugs and went to jail. They do know, however, if you have Jesus in your heart, soul and mind, and if you love them.

Serving the poor and the homeless is an exercise in not finding faults in others.

"Do not judge, or you too will be judged. For in the same way you judge others, you will be judged..." (Matthew 7:1, 2)

Don't tell them they are drinking, or whatever their sin is... they know. Would you tell a man in a wheelchair, "Hey, your legs don't work. You're handicapped!" God forbid!

Don't take for granted that they are homeless or are hungry or need you at all. Don't think you're their "savior." Some have been surviving well for years in the street without you. Ask first, "Can you use some food? Are you hungry?" Be respectful. Don't suddenly jump on them to help them. Ask politely. Respect their personal dignity.

Do not approach the least of these quickly, especially if there are more than one of you ministering. Don't approach them suddenly or hastily. Many homeless are used to being alone and may feel threatened by quickly approaching people.

Don't introduce yourself. Your name is irrelevant. You are there to promote the Name of Jesus, not yourself. If they don't see Jesus through you, it's because there is still too much of you to see - less of you and more of Jesus. In approaching Goliath, David did not say, "I am David, son of Jesse!" No, he did not give his name, but instead announced himself as coming "in the name of the Lord Almighty, the God of the armies of Israel..." (1 Samuel 17:45). And God gave him the victory.

Don't talk about yourself. You are there to talk about them and hopefully they will see Jesus in you.

Don't tell them what church you belong to. You did not come in the name of a church but in the Name of Jesus. Jesus sent you, not your church.

Don't bind them up in your social norms and so take them away from the liberty they have had in the street.

Don't take pictures unless you ask first.

Don't tell them to clean up their camp or do it for them.

Do not give them beer, cigarettes, alcohol, knives, etc.

Don't ask where they are staying or where they are going.

Don't ask them where their camp is or where they are staying at night. As night time is a very vulnerable time, they are very guarded about where they sleep. Be patient. And why do you need that information, anyhow? It is better to ask, "Do you have a safe place to sleep at night where you are dry?" It shows more care and concern. They will volunteer the "where" if they so choose. Don't push. Show yourself to be the concerned person that you are.

Don't start preaching to them the first time you meet. In fact, don't preach to them at all unless they invite you to hold services for them.

Do not go see them every day of the week. Once or twice a week is good. You may see them more if you are driving one or another to appointments or if you have business to take care of with them. Do not overstay your welcome in a camp. When you are done visiting, ministering, feeding, praying, etc., say good-bye. Sometimes they will feel like talking more than other times. Be sensitive to different camps who may or may not want your extended presence. Some camps are more social than others. Once they get their "drunk on", it's time to leave!

Don't get there too late on Saturday (or any day) to minister to them, as they start to get their "drunk on" at about three in the afternoon and begin to be useless as far as Godly conversation is concerned.

Don't use a credit card to purchase items for the "least of these." Don't use money you don't have to help them. Trust the Lord.

Don't give them cash. It is preferable to take care of their needs with the purchase of physical items that you give them. If they need medication, take them to the pharmacy and pay there. If they need gas, bring them some or take them to the gas station.

Cash may be misused. If you must give cash, do not give over five dollars.

Do not bring up the subject of their family unless they bring it up first. I have heard so many horrendous stories of painful, dysfunctional families. It pains them, and it most often is the reason why they are where they are. If you had been rejected as a youth as they were, your low self-esteem might make you want to be homeless, also. However, Jesus is not a respecter of persons. The homeless are loved by the Lord, and they will probably hold a higher position in heaven than most because of their child-like faith!

Do not push them to come out of their circumstances. But, rather, train them to be useful to the Lord in their circumstances - to minister to others. We cannot measure everyone according to our own lifestyle. They will tell you when they are ready to change, and you can then help them. The homeless can be your friends when you meet them on their terms, where they're at. Don't expect them to come up to your social standard, where you're at.

Do not house any of them in your home. They are not used to your lifestyle and will not be able to adjust. Do not go there.

Do not be negative as you minister to the "least of these." Stay positive. They already have enough negative things in their life.

Do not give them your phone number unless you want them to call you! They will call you. If they need to go to an appointment, then fine, let them call you. You may give your number if you have known them for a while and trust them not to misuse it.

Don't take over their life.

Do not get into a routine of doing the same thing every week, out of habit. Remember the reason you are amongst the "least of these;" their spiritual welfare.

Do listen to a homeless man if he tells you not to go to a certain camp. He knows something you don't. There may be drugs or crime present.

Do share with them one different scripture every week.

Do let them know that they are in the family of God.

Do love the poor with all your heart, all your might, all your mind and all your soul, as you would love Jesus, himself.

Do talk with them to find out where they're at, what they need, how they're doing.

Do get to know their heart, their needs, their faith and their names.

Do use alcohol sanitizer or wipes between visits for the sake of all involved.

Do be consistent in your visits, in what you bring for them, in your care and love for them. If you have established rapport, then ask them if they are saved and if you can pray for them before you leave. However, let the Holy Spirit guide you also.

Do feed them and minister to them even if they do not thank you or if you feel they may be too drunk to remember your act of kindness. Your love will touch them and spark deep within their heart the fire of God; that is, revival.

Do pray, pray, pray, pray, pray, pray, pray, pray... Spend lots of time with Jesus.

Do disciple the poor and the homeless. Teach and encourage them to tell others how Jesus has taken care of them and blessed them. Teach them to remind the others that Jesus loves them and died on the cross for them so they may be saved and have all their sins forgiven. Let them know to give thanks at all times, for He is God.

Do tell them to love one another, especially if they start belittling other homeless persons. When they start the blame game or the bitter game, don't go there. Love them unconditionally and teach them to do likewise.

Do provide enough for all of the needy you are seeing at one time. Don't buy three of something when you know there will be twenty people you will be with that day. It will seem like you are showing favoritism.

Do remain calm if the police approach you while ministering to the homeless. I have seen many very loving, kindhearted officers who care for the homeless. However, there are also a few who have it out for the homeless. In hating the homeless, they show that they are really hating themselves. Pray for peace in that officer's heart. Pray a blessing on the rest.

Do keep your eyes open when you pray. I have never read in the Word of God that Jesus ever closed His eyes when praying for others. In fact, it was the opposite - He kept them open when praying for others. Not only do you want to see how God is answering your prayer, but you need to see what is going on around you; and you want to see the reaction of the person for whom you are praying. Are they receiving your prayer? Are they getting healed? Praying for others is not a time to close your eyes. You are a soldier of God; do not close your eyes and do not be "slain" in the spirit. Good soldiers "stand" tall and "see" well, both winning characteristics of Gideon's 300, and why God picked them to show His glory and awesome power.

Do keep your prayers short. Remember, the more you say, the less you mean. Attention span in the street for prayers is about fifteen SECONDS. At twenty seconds it begins to be too long, and you start to lose them. God understands. He hears you. Stop praying at fifteen seconds then go home in your prayer closet and finish your long prayer for that needy "least of these."

Do take time out for yourself. Don't feel guilty. You need it. Have someone else handle your job while you're gone. They could probably use the experience of ministering without you being present. It's good for you, and it's good for them.

Part 2

Other Folds

This book is not geared to the homeless alone, for the "least of these" extend to many other people. Believe me when I say that there are millions upon millions of other people who fall in the category of the "least of these." After all, who has not been the "least of these" at one time or another? At the time of this writing, a horrendous typhoon (hurricane) hit the Philippine Islands and suddenly over a million people are homeless. The "least of these" can appear suddenly and at any given place or time.

There is part of our aged population to consider as the "least of these." Most of the world respects those who have attained old age and see them as a source of wisdom. That is hardly true in America where seniors may feel more discarded rather than sought after for wisdom. If history is your interest, minister to a person over the age of eighty years old and learn wisdom someone else has paid the price to learn.

It may not necessarily be a matter of finances for our older generation, but rather of physical limitations. They may be financially stable but not able to get around as they used to. You may be able to drive them to necessary appointments and minister the love of Jesus to them. EVERYONE, no matter what their circumstances, needs the love of Jesus in their life.

Seniors may also have a need for food because they may not be able to afford it or because they are too sick, weak or frail to fix it themselves. There are organizations in place where you can volunteer, such as Meals on Wheels. You can also start ministering on your own to those in your neighborhood circle and then grow into your city circle. As long as you minister to at least one of the "least of these," you've dared to go beyond the church walls and into the street. Now, go and minister to two...and three...and so on.

Seniors can also be helped with house repairs, mowing lawns, house cleaning and pet care. However, you will find that the biggest need of the elderly, whether in their home or especially in nursing homes, is plain 'ol fellowship time. Visit them; sit down and spend time with them; love on them; testify about Jesus; and bring them a little something you found out they would like to have. And no matter how old they are, pray for their healing. Be consistent, and one day God's anointing will fall on you and you will be instrumental in seniors being able to walk out of nursing homes totally healed!

There are also children's ministries available. In all the ministering I have done to children in my life, I have found the one thing they want the most. It does not matter where in the world you may find them. It matters not the socio-economic level in which they find themselves. They will forsake everything else, even their very own life, in order to acquire this thing which they need most. Many children of all ages attempt suicide because this "thing" is missing from their life. If you can give it to them, you will never lack to have at least one child wrapped around your neck, hugging you tight and not letting you go. It's this thing called Love - God's love through you. They know if you have it, and they will make a beeline to you to get it!

You can substitute teach, be a teacher's assistant or teacher's aide. Teachers would love to have you in their classroom. Also, you can take care of children in your home. Yes, you get paid for these things, but that allows you to minister the love of Jesus to children. You can tutor young children and teenagers. You can be a foster parent or a child advocate. You can be a Big Brother or Big Sister or mentor a child. All these ministries will allow a child to receive much needed, esteem-building love in their life.

I will not bore you with the reams of statistics about the millions upon millions of needy children in the United States. Believe me, you don't have to go overseas to a third world country to see hungry children who also need love, clothing and shelter. I can testify to you from firsthand account, from what I have seen with my own eyes in our country, in our cities, in our neighborhoods and in our schools; there are starving children near you. I minister to children in our county public schools and I personally deal first hand with homelessness, hunger, and poverty in our classrooms - in this beautiful vacation destination by the beach! Thank God we have in our city so many who give to the needy.

There is not a country in the world, not a city or a neighborhood which is exempt from the presence of the "least of these." Truly, the harvest is ripe throughout the world, starting in your own neighborhood.

You can make up food bags for school children to take home on Fridays after school (The Backpack Club). There are children who eat very little again until Monday morning when they get back to school and have breakfast. You can provide school supplies, shoes, school shirts, bikes, Christmas presents...the list is endless.

Find a struggling family with children in your neighborhood and make sure they get help with food or other need. There may be single parent homes who desperately need any food you may be able to offer...and clothing...and love. Hopefully, they are getting food stamps. If not, you can help them apply. Ask the Lord to show you where the need is. He will lead you to the proper place where you can minister the healing love of Jesus Christ.

Someone called me yesterday because there was a dad with a seven-year old living under a bridge in thirty-five degree weather. The child was not attending school. This was in my own town, in America, in 2013! Always be ready with the knowledge of resources available for when the "least of these" are in need. Do you know where the Food Stamp Office is? Where can they get assistance for health care, utilities, rent, food, identification? Where are shelters for men or women with children? How do you contact the Department of Social Services in your area? Where can they get a meal? Where is the Employment Office? And don't forget; pray, pray, pray!

Many times, you may not receive because you simply don't ask.

The Lord has made you such that your gifts allow you to do well in a particular ministry. So, certainly, the Lord's guidance should be sought. He already has a ministry to the "least of these" for you. You already feel that you emphasize with one group, or another. You were born for that particular purpose. Your empathy for that category of the "least of these" will guide you to fill their needs with a heart full of love. You will bless the Lord Jesus Christ, and revival will ensue (follow). Glory to God.

"If you do away with the yoke of oppression, with the pointing finger and malicious talk, and if you spend yourselves in behalf of the hungry and satisfy the needs of the oppressed, then your light will rise in the darkness, and your night will become like the noonday. The Lord will guide you always; he will satisfy your needs in a sun-scorched land and will strengthen your frame." (Isaiah 58:9-11)

CHAPTER *fifteen*

How Do I Get A Big Heart Full Of Love?

Part 1

Is Love A Gift?

Please read this chapter very carefully, for without love, you have no ministry. Read it more than once, until you know for sure where and how to get more of this amazing, deep, Godly love.

"Because of the increase of wickedness, the love of most will grow cold..." (Matthew 24:12)

The above scripture chapter concerns the signs of the end of the age - the coming of Jesus to meet us in the air. What will he find on earth at that time? He will find much wickedness and very little love. Have you noticed we are presently in that age? There is, however, a remnant chosen by grace (Romans 11:5) who will exhibit that precious end-time gem called love. There will be a few who will forsake the world, carry their cross, die daily and who, against all odds, will be enabled by the Lord God to love as Jesus loved. That's you!

What I "think," or what my "opinion" is on this subject of love is totally irrelevant. Love is such an important subject in your life and your eternity that you must adhere (that means stick like glue) strictly to the Scriptures for understanding. God is love. Don't go anywhere else for understanding of love.

"Whoever does not love does not know God, because God is love." (1 John 4:8)

Ouch! That's kind of blunt. But I didn't say it; God said it through His Word. The best way to get to know God is to grow in His love in you and through you. Submit to the Author of Love for understanding of love.

"And he has given us this command: Whoever loves God must also love his brother." (1 John 4:21)

"We know that we have passed from death to life, because we love our brothers. Anyone who does not love remains in death." (1 John 3:14)

Double ouch! If you in your heart do not truly love your fellow man, you may not be saved and may still be living in death! Of course, whether you can love or not doesn't decide if you are saved. You know that you are saved by grace. But by your Christ-like love others can see if you are saved because love is a fruit of the spirit.

"But the fruit of the Spirit is love...those who belong to Christ Jesus have crucified the sinful nature with its passions and desires." (Galatians 5:22, 24)

"... (If I) have not love, I am nothing...I gain nothing." (1 Corinthians 13:2, 3)

When you are not loving in the name of Jesus, the world looks at you but does not see the love of Christ in your heart which is proclaimed so often and so loudly by Christians. To the world, the love you exhibit is a gauge of Christ in you. Therefore:

"A new command I give you: Love one another. As I have loved you, so you must love one another. By this all men will know that you are my disciples, if you love one another." (John 13:34)

All men - the whole world - will know that you are disciples of Jesus Christ, the Lord of All, if they see that you at least love other Christians. Love the brothers (and sisters, of course) as Jesus loved you and died for you. Here comes the subject of the cross again! You will not only carry your cross, but you will die on it (the world in you). Less of you, more of Jesus. But there is more...

"...live a life of love, just as Christ loved us and gave himself up for us as a fragrant offering and sacrifice." (Ephesians 5:2)

Jesus wants you to follow in His footsteps because He wants you to be like Him. As the Father sent Him, He sends you. Yes, saints of God, you must offer yourself up for others (the saved and unsaved) as an acceptable sacrifice. More of Him, less of you. Do you want to be part of the coming ground roots revival or do you just want to sit on your easy chair and watch it pass you by? Paul was wanting to explain unity in love:

"My purpose is that they (the saints) **may be encouraged in heart and united in love..." (Colossians 2:2)**

Your purpose must be to encourage and unite the saints of God in love. This happens throughout your day as you meet, work and speak with the saints. However, it especially comes into being at your home meetings where, being united in love, God answers your prayers and gives you understanding, wisdom and knowledge. You cannot do this alone; you need fellowship with the other saints of God. This unity of love is also manifested in the street, as you minister to the "least of these."

"And over all these virtues put on love, which binds them all together in perfect unity." (Colossians 3:14)

"...make my joy complete by being like-minded, having the same love, being one is spirit and purpose." (Philippians 2:2)

How will the Lord find His Bride at His second coming? Will she be scattered like wind-blown sand in the desert? Or will all the saints be bound together by deep love and unity? Once you have become able to love within your inner circle (home meetings, neighborhood), it is then time to move to your outer circles (your city):

"May the Lord make your love increase and overflow for each other and for everyone else..." (1 Thessalonians 3:12)

"But I tell you: Love your enemies...If you love those who love you, what reward will you get?" (Matthew 5:44, 46)

By now you are probably saying, "Yes, I'll die on the cross daily for the ones I love...but my enemies?" Remember, you were an enemy of God, once. When you were at your worst in your life, they were driving the nails in His hands. When you were most sinful and hateful, He was dying on the cross because He loved you. Jesus wants you to love others as He loved you.

You are saved by grace and will spend eternity in heaven. But when you get to heaven, you will be rewarded according to your deeds while you were on earth. Seek to be filled with His love for the unsaved; seek Godly unity with the saints; seek to serve Him in Word and in power. The reward you get is for eternity. Carrying your cross is but a temporary price for an eternal reward. It is comparable to the prick of the immunization needle which will then protect you for life.

"For the Son of Man is going to come in his Father's glory with his angels, and then he will reward each person according to what he has done." (Matthew 16:27)

God does not tell you to do something that you cannot do. If He tells you to do something, it's because He has made a way for you to do it. So, how can you love as Jesus loved you? Where and how do you get this love?

"In love a throne will be established...one from the house of David..." (Isaiah 16:5)

Part 2

Can't Buy You Love

Is Godly love in and through you a free gift, like the gifts of teaching, preaching or music? The answer to this question is a resounding NO!

If you are saved and want to love as Jesus loved, it will cost you a trip to the cross - yours. If you want God's love to touch others through you, you will earn it. You must shed the ways of the world which insist on clinging to every fiber of your being, and preventing you from loving deeply with the love of Jesus. Separating yourself from the ways of the world is NOT a painless process, but the reward is an unprecedented (never seen before) closeness to your Lord Jesus Christ.

"This is how we know what love is: Jesus Christ laid down his life for us. And we ought to lay down our lives for our brothers." (1 John 3:16)

"Flee the evil desires of youth, and pursue...love." (2 Timothy 2:22)

There will come a point in your walk with the Lord when shallow, worldly love is no longer expressed in you. Jesus himself, loving through you, will bring healing to all those you touch with that true love now within you. Every time a part of you dies, more of you becomes alive. That is, more of Christ becomes alive in you for His will to be done through you. More of Jesus, less of you.

"No, none has ever seen God; but if we love one another, God lives in us and his love is made complete in us." (1 John 4:12)

True love will be given to you by the Lord so you may serve Him more. More love will not be given to you if you just sit on the sofa at home or on a pew in church. If you want to go out and minister to the "least of these," the Lord will gradually fill you with more and more love to allow your ministry to not only grow, but become more powerful.

"Dear friends, let us love one another, for love comes from God." (1 John 4:7)

True love comes from God. He has an unlimited amount for even the hardest of hearts. The more you pray for love and the more you serve Him according to His will, the more love He will pour out in you. Your growth in Godly love is directly proportional to how much of self you let go. God will help you get rid of worldly junk in your heart so he can replace it with His supernatural love.

"...love...comes from a pure heart and a good conscience and a sincere faith." (1 Timothy 1:5)

In order to get love, you also need faith - sincere faith. You pray to God with a purity of purpose, with faith, and God will give you love. He wants to give you love. After all, He IS love. Since He created you in His image, He wants you to be like Him; God also wants you to BE love. So, when you are praying for love from God, you are praying according to God's will and He has to answer you. You will get love!

"And I pray that you, being rooted and established in love, may have power, together with all the saints, to grasp how wide and long and high and deep is the love of Christ, and to know this love that surpasses knowledge - that you may be filled to the measure of all the fullness of God." (Ephesians 3:17-19)

As you grow in love by reading the Word, serving Him and coming to him in prayer, little by little He will let you have this love that surpasses human knowledge. Over time, He will fill you with as much love as you can handle. As you seek to be in God's heart (in His presence) power and love will grow in your heart.

"And this is my prayer: That your love may abound more and more...so that you may be able to discern what is best and may be pure and blameless until the day of Christ..." (Philippians 1:9)

Here, Paul was praying that you would grow in God's love. So if you want that love that surpasses knowledge, asking (praying) for it is essential. Not only your prayers, but the prayers of others. Hence, the home meetings where the saints of God can be encouraged and can pray for each other and grow in God's love and in unity. Hear me, saints of God, the Lord has THE PERFECT PLAN!

To summarize how to get filled to the brim with God's love, I have listed ten points as explained above:
1. Godly love in and through you is not a free gift.
2. Getting this love will cost you.

3. You will have to carry your cross
4. You will need to shed the world (crucify the flesh).
5. When part of you dies, more of you lives.
6. True love only comes from God.
7. You have to ask God in faith and sincerity for His love to abide in you.
8. God fills you with His love gradually.
9. Pray, pray, pray, pray, pray, pray, pray...
10. Go and minister in the Name of Jesus Christ.

"...for you yourselves have been taught by God to love each other...yet we urge you, brothers, to do so more and more." (1 Thessalonians 4:9, 10)

CHAPTER *sixteen*

Salvation, Baptism And The Glory

Part 1

How Do You Bring Someone To Salvation?

Thank God that while the world gets more complicated, the message of hope in Christ Jesus and salvation is just as simple as ever. Children as young as four years old "get saved." In fact, you cannot show understanding of a spiritual principle unless you can explain it to a ten year old. The "least of these," the little children of God that they are, are in a position to more easily understand the message of salvation.

"I tell you the truth, anyone who will not receive the kingdom of God like a little child will never enter it." (Luke 18:17)

Jesus was sent to preach salvation to all men, but especially to the poor.

"The Spirit of the Lord is on me, because he has anointed me to preach good news to the poor." (Luke 4:18)

"Blessed are you who are poor, for yours is the kingdom of God. Blessed are you who hunger now, for you will be satisfied." (Luke 6:20, 21)

"Go back and report to John what you have seen and heard... the good news is preached to the poor." (Luke 7:22)

No wonder this coming great revival will rise up from the street. That's where the greatest concentration of the poor is found. Isn't that where Jesus' ministry was - in the street? Didn't they then have the greatest revival the world had ever seen? So it shall be again. It started in the street, and it will end in the street.

The first person Jesus "saved" while on earth was one of the "least of these." This unsaved man was a prisoner being put to death for his crime. Prisoners are also considered to be the "least of these," since Jesus said He was sent to proclaim freedom for the prisoners **(Luke 4:18)**. If you have a prison ministry, you are ministering to the "least of these."

Jesus must have ministered to this man at some time or another; this man must have heard the plan of salvation. In an ironic twist of events, both Jesus and this man were being executed at the same time. Jesus was innocent, but this man was guilty. Jesus was there because of love; the man was there because of sin.

"One of the criminals who hung there hurled insults at him: 'Aren't you the Christ? Save yourself and us!'" (Luke 23:39)

Evidently, the criminal (thief) on the cross had hurled insults which were not recorded in the bible. His tone of voice must have been such that we understand he was not repentant at all. He was in pain; he had just been whipped, shredded, beat and hung on a cross to die. He was in no mood to discuss salvation theology and be repentant. Instead of saying, "You are the

Christ," he showed doubt by asking a question instead. Doubt doesn't do your salvation any good because you are saved by faith...in Jesus Christ!

"But the other criminal rebuked him. 'Don't you fear God,' he said, 'since you are under the same sentence? We are punished justly, for we are getting what our deeds deserve. But this man has done nothing wrong.'" (v. 40, 41)

The second criminal being hung on his cross was in the same misery as the other, but...he feared God. He admitted being guilty, a sinner, and being justly punished, deserving death (as do all humans). He also confessed that Jesus was innocent. This man must have also seen Jesus' miracles and heard His teaching. He might have figured out that Jesus not only did nothing wrong, but was sinless. The next line hints that he maybe considered Jesus to be the Messiah, the Christ, the Savior, God in person.

"Then he said, 'Jesus, remember me when you come into your kingdom.'" (v. 42)

During the last, intensely painful moment of his life, he finally had faith that Jesus had power over death and eternity. In his situation he might have been delirious, which makes us think that he may have heard of Jesus' ministry somewhat before he was jailed and maybe had pondered it and understood some of it. Now that he was about to die, he realized the decision had to be made.

Fear God...believe in Jesus as the Messiah...be set free...live forever...by faith... do it now.

He believed.

"Jesus answered him, "I tell you the truth, today you will be with me in paradise." (v. 43)

Though three more hours of horrific agony would go by, that man's eternity was sealed. Jesus, the perfect sacrifice, knew He would die before that man would and so could offer him paradise (heaven). A criminal on death row was the first recorded salvation in the bible. Jesus' blood (death) on the cross paid the price for that man's freedom. That criminal was "saved" from eternal death in Hell. The Son of God had given him free passage to heaven, to eternity with God. That man believed in Jesus Christ and confessed (acknowledged out loud) that Jesus had power over death and eternity; in fact, that Jesus was God.

"He (the Lord) will be the sure foundation for your times, a rich store of salvation and wisdom and knowledge; the fear of the Lord is the key to this treasure." (Isaiah 33:6)

The reason Jesus could give that man such deliverance was because He knew his heart. He knew of that man's sincerity and faith. By confessing his belief in four sentences, that man was saved. Will the same scenario happen for all? No! But the criminal, now made pure and holy, did two things all sinners must do to be saved;

"...if you confess with your mouth, 'Jesus is Lord,' and believe in your heart that God raised him from the dead, you will be saved." (Romans 10:9)

Jesus did not say to that criminal, "Repeat after me the sinner's prayer..." Or, "Now, we have to find a way to baptize you!" Or, "Now, we have to find you a church to go to!" Or, "Wait, you have to fill out this card!"

No, that's it! That same day that criminal found himself in heaven for eternity. We just tore out 11,294 pages out of your man-authored theology textbook!

"No, wait a minute," you say! "We have to say, 'Jesus is the Son of God, died and was resurrected on the third day'...and...and... you have to ask forgiveness for all your sins...and...and you have to get on your knees...and cry... yes...you have to cry...with snot running out of your nose and all!"

Nope!

Neither is there any scriptural support for you to tell anyone, "To be saved, you must ask Jesus to come into your heart."

Nope!

After a man (or woman) FIRST believes, Jesus will THEN come into that believer's heart. Jesus has already fulfilled His commitment to mankind on the cross. Then, a man fulfills his part of the covenant by BELIEVING in Jesus. Don't let a man belittle our Lord Jesus Christ by commanding Him to come into his heart! Instead, fear God, have faith, let a man humble himself and believe Jesus is Lord, and he will be saved. THEN, Jesus will come and dwell in that man's heart.

If one lives more than three hours after salvation, then there are some things with which you should follow through. Yes, baptism is one of them. YOU baptize them! ANYONE WHO IS SAVED CAN BAPTIZE THE SAVED!

Here's what you say when you baptize someone (in pool, river, lake, ocean).

You, the baptizer, ask the baptizee; *"Do you___(name)___ by faith believe in Jesus Christ as your Lord and Savior, and confess Him publicly?"*

The answer must be yes!

Then you say; *"I now baptize you in the name of the Father, the Son and the Holy Spirit."*

Dunk.

If in the days of Noah, God had wanted to baptize by sprinkling, He would have rained a few drops on them, and that would have done it. However, God let it rain heavy so as to flood (immerse) everything under water!

If John the Baptist had wanted to baptize by sprinkling, all he would have needed in that hot desert was a cup of water, and that would have done it. Instead, he found where the Jordan River ran deep enough to dunk, and he stood in the middle of it baptizing!

Immersion, saints of God, immersion.

That's another 3,782 pages in your man-authored theology textbook you can rip out. At one of your home meetings, you all can pray about, research in the bible and discuss "baptism."

Are there more explanations about salvation? Yes. As **Romans 10:9** continues...

"For it is with your heart that you believe and are justified, and it is with your mouth that you confess and are saved. As the Scripture says, 'Anyone who trusts in him will never be put to shame...' the same Lord is Lord of all and richly blesses all who call on him, for, 'Everyone who calls on the name of the Lord will be saved.'" (Romans 10:10-13)

Justified means: the criminal on the cross was declared supernaturally guiltless or blameless; he was now in a personal and right relationship with God.

Is there more? Oh, yes, lots and lots more wonderful revelations in the Word of God concerning our miraculous salvation. If the person you lead to salvation should live more than three hours, he will have a lifetime of learning ahead of him, and he will **"grow in his salvation" (1 Peter 2:3).**

To make your search on salvation easier, here is a list of a few relevant scriptures you can look up during a home meeting. Understand salvation thoroughly, but continue to keep it simple.

2 Cor. 5:20, 21; Acts 2:38, 10:43, 26:20; Romans 5:8, 11, 21, 6:7, 23, 8:1, 14, 17, 34;

1 John 4:15, 5:1; 1 Peter 2:24; Ephesians 2:5, 8, 9; John 3:16; Matt. 16:27

**"Salvation is found in no one else, for there is no other name under heaven given to men by which we must be saved."
(Acts 4:12)**

Part 2

Oh, The Glory!

"...everyone who is called by my name, whom *I created for my glory*, whom I formed and made." (Isaiah 43:7)

God created you to glorify Him. Why would he do that? All of heaven worships and glorifies God. All the Elders, all the creatures of heaven, all the angels, the whole universe gives glory to God. If he receives so much glory in heaven, then why does he value us humans on a speck of dust in this universe? This is why; because you are the only ones amongst all of God's creation who glorify Him...BY FAITH, not having seen Him.

"From one man He made every nation of men, that they should inhabit the whole earth...God did this so that men would seek Him and perhaps reach out for Him and find Him..." (Acts 17:26, 27)

We who are called by His Name are so unique in the universe that...

"Even angels long to look into these things." (1 Peter 1:12)

All who exist in heaven are continually before the Lord. All heavenly beings have face to face time with God. They see Him, talk to Him, worship Him and they have beheld His glory since the day they were created. If we were to look at God's glory for just a split second, the overwhelming power of it would kill us because we have carnal rather than spiritual bodies. That is by design. We are the only created beings that do not see God, AND YET BELIEVE in Him. To God, that is very special, and He brags about us to the heavenly beings **(Job 1:8)**. We are a very peculiar people in all of God's realm. Glory to God!

"But you are a chosen people, a royal priesthood, a holy nation, a people belonging to God, that you may declare the praises (glory) **of him who called you out of darkness into his wonderful light** (glory)**." (1 Peter 2:9)**

You are a peculiar people, and since you are saved you have a priestly call on your life. In fact, we are so special to God that we will judge the world when Jesus establishes His kingdom on Earth **(1 Corinthians 6:2). Don't you also know that we will judge angels (v. 3)?**

My concern, at this point, is how your ministry relates to the subject of "the glory of God." We are going to look at a very narrow slice of the glory pie, a very narrow focus of the subject. We are concerned with your ministry and how it relates to the glory of God. Declare the glory that God deserves and watch your ministry grow. Exalt (praise or glorify) His Holy Name and you, saints of God, will also grow in Holy Spirit power. Glorify God and His Son Jesus in all that you do.

Glory: Hebrew, *kabod*; Greek, *doxa*; honor, splendor, wealth, high status, dignity, brilliance; praise: the awesome light that radiates from God's presence and is associated with His acts of power. Here are some things you do that give God glory:

"...glorify him (God) with thanksgiving." (Psalm 69:30)

"May God...give you a spirit of unity...so that you may glorify the God and Father of our Lord Jesus Christ." (Romans 15:5, 6)

"...glorify God for his mercy..." (Romans 15:9)

"Live such good lives that...they may see your good deeds and glorify God..." (1 Peter 2:12)

"This is to my Father's glory, that you bear much fruit..." (John 15:8)

"I have brought you glory on earth by completing the work you gave me to do." (John 17:4)

"And glory has come to me (Jesus) through them (you)." (John 17:10)

"Fear God and give him glory." (Revelation 14:7)

"Let us rejoice and be glad and give him glory!" (Revelation 19:7)

It is not even within our present, earthly status to imagine what the glory of God is like. Though God wants us to try, no words, pictures, paintings, songs or any other form of human expression can adequately describe it. However, God wanted the world to both see His glory and yet still believe in Him by faith. How can that be achieved while we are still in our carnal bodies? God so loved the world that He sent His Son, God in person, so we may behold His glory. Jesus said;

"Anyone who has seen me has seen the Father." (John 14:9)

From beginning to end, the entire bible points to Jesus, and the glory of God. As if that wasn't enough, man has seen fit to write enumerable (impossible to count) amount of books on the subject of the glory of God. However, it is always important to return to the source of spiritual knowledge - the Word of God. Though you may have looked at a scripture a dozen times, go back over it again. Study it, search it out and pray over it because the interpretation of the scriptures is of the Holy Spirit.

For example, let us find something exciting about the results of glorifying God:

"I tell you the truth, anyone who has faith in me will do what I have been doing. He will do even greater things than these, because I am going to the Father." (John 14:12)

We love to hear this scripture because it is a very exciting promise. We hope in it. Yes, we have heard stories past of great saints of God who have done such "greater" things. But you, yourself, know the bulk of this promise has yet to come to pass in the last days in order to bring in the last great harvest, the fullness of the gentiles. God is the God of timing and to attempt action out of timing with the Lord is to invite failure. Is there something we are missing?

Yes, the glory of the Lord.

As with often quoted scripture, it is too easy to have only partial understanding. Therefore, we must continue reading to see what we are missing, as it may be the piece of the puzzle that holds us back from the completion of God's will in our life.

"And I will do whatever you ask in my name, so that the Son may bring glory to the Father. You may ask me for anything in my name, and I will do it." (v. 13)

You see, Jesus will do whatever you ask. But why would He do that? So the Son may bring GLORY to the Father. Will the answers to all your prayers glorify the name of Jesus? When you pray, do you say to yourself, "I pray this because the answer will glorify You, O Lord?"

"This, the first of his miraculous signs, Jesus performed at Cana in Galilee. He thus revealed his glory, and his disciples put their faith in him." (John 2:11)

The reason for the necessity of God's glory in your ministry is so that others may put their faith in Jesus. Remember, none of the glory goes to you. Jesus gets on hundred percent of all the glory. Your service to God and the miracles, signs and wonders manifested in you are there to glorify the Lord our God. They are not for your entertainment or for your own glory. God forbid!

"This sickness will not end in death. No, it is for God's glory so that God's Son may be glorified through it." (John 11:4)

There is a vast theological discussion possible here, but I did tell you we are looking at a very thin slice of the pie; the slice that keeps your ministry empowered. The Lord says, "This sickness." This does not mean "all" sickness. Much sickness is brought on by sin or demonic possession or influence. However, "this" particular sickness was to glorify Jesus so that God may be glorified.

When you give food to the homeless, you give it to Jesus. If you can do that, then Jesus is glorified. If Jesus is glorified in this simple act, God is glorified also. If you keep on glorifying Jesus, God will want to bless you more because he loves for His human creation to glorify His Holy Name. The more you glorify God with the little things, the more He will give to you until there comes a time when signs, miracles and wonders through you will glorify the Lord even more.

Don't pray, "...so your glory may be seen" as a mindless repetitive addition to every prayer. Get back in "your little circle," and then in your larger circle (home meetings), and make sure you understand the deeper meaning of "glorifying" the Holy Name of Jesus Christ. You'll find out more and more that it's not about you, but about the Lord. Your ministry is not a selfish endeavor which glorifies you. God forbid! Do not get giddy or overly happy about yourself when you have done something good for the "least of these," and forget to give ALL glory to God.

Do you think it might have something to do with carrying your cross? Less of you and more of Jesus? It is so easy to start taking credit for a successful ministry. You must continually guard against pride which so easily sneaks into your heart. You'll be reminded again and again to carry your daily cross, to crucify the flesh, to give all glory to God from the very depth of your soul. How serious are you about serving your Lord Jesus?

"I have been crucified with Christ and I no longer live, but Christ lives in me. The life I live in the body, I live by faith in the Son of God, who loved me and gave himself for me." (Galatians 2:20)

"Since we live by the Spirit, let us keep in step with the Spirit. Let us not become conceited, provoking and envying each other." (Galatians 5:25, 26)

The ministry of our Lord Jesus Christ is not a competitive sport! We must unite in love, giving ALL glory to God the Father, not putting our desires first, but making our heart's desire God's will to be accomplished in our life. At one point, God will see that you are ready, and He will anoint you with that radical, Holy Spirit, miracle working anointing identified with Jesus Christ, the First Begotten Son of the living God.

"He called you to this through our gospel, that you might share in the glory of our Lord Jesus Christ." (2 Thessalonians 2:14)

"...whatever you do, do it all for the glory of God." (1 Corinthians 10:31)

CHAPTER *seventeen*

The Anointing

Part 1

Power To Fulfill Your Ministry

God is the only one who decides that you should get an anointing. Your pastor does not do that. The church leadership does not do that. Man does not do that. God may send a man to tell you about your anointing, to manifest it to you. He may not. He may send someone to lay hands on you or anoint you with oil to receive that anointing. Or, it may just be between God and you. The anointing may suddenly come upon you to immediately empower you. Alternatively, it may take years to develop the qualities needed to fulfill the anointing that you have received.

For King Saul, the anointing worked immediately:

"Then Samuel took a flask of oil and poured it on Saul's head and kissed him, saying, 'Has not the Lord anointed you leader over his inheritance?'...The Spirit of the Lord will come upon you in power, and you...will be changed into a different person...do whatever your hand finds to do, for God is with you." (1 Samuel 10:1, 6)

David was anointed at a young age to become king.

"So Samuel took the horn of oil and anointed him (David)**... and from that day on the Spirit of the Lord came upon David in power." (1 Samuel 16:13)**

However, contrary to Saul's anointing, it took David fifteen years to ascend to the throne and fulfill his anointing. It took him that long, according to God's time, for David to develop into the man he needed to become to be an effective king; a man after God's own heart.

What is an "anointing?" What does it mean?

Anointing: (New Testament) Greek, *chrio:* to assign a person to a special task, implying a giving of power by God to accomplish the task.

Anointing: (Old Testament) Hebrew, *masah*: usually referring to the pouring or smearing of sacred oil on a person in a ceremony of dedication, symbolizing divine empowering to accomplish the task or office.

You are saved by grace and filled with the Holy Spirit. The Holy Spirit teaches you to be like Jesus and guides you throughout your life. However, if you are going to give yourself over completely to your God-given ministry, sooner or later, the Lord will anoint you with power to fulfill that ministry.

The anointing is to have your gifts fully manifested and to be empowered from the Lord Jesus Christ for the purpose of accomplishing your ministry. I guarantee you will then (as Saul did) feel like a different person. When you first receive your supernatural anointing from the Lord, your exceedingly great joy may make you feel like you can float or fly in the air! At first, you may feel so much exhilaration in the Holy Spirit that you may have a hard time containing your excitement.

(On the same day, after Saul's anointing) **"The Spirit of God came upon him in power, and he joined in their prophesying. When all those who had known him saw him prophesying with the prophets, they asked each other, 'What is this that has happened to the son of Kish? Is Saul also among the prophets?'"** (1 Samuel 10:10, 11)

However, know that it is possible to receive the anointing, say, "Thank you, Jesus," and just keep on working as if the anointing had always been there. At that point, though, your ministry will become more powerful. You will find yourself being able to accomplish more than you had before.

The Lord may reshape your heart so that whatever you do in that ministry will be God working through you.

"As Saul turned to leave Samuel, God changed Saul's heart... that day (after being anointed)." (1 Samuel 10:9)

Be forewarned, ALL glory MUST go to God! One hundred percent! The anointing may make you feel very confident in accomplishing its purpose. Do NOT get overconfident. Be thankful to God at ALL times for that anointing. It is your purpose to HUMBLY glorify God with your anointing. God will be with you in power. Do as He tells you. Do not brag about your anointing. Do not abuse that anointing or you may lose it, as King Saul sadly did later on by disobeying God **(1 Samuel 15:8-15)**.

At this point, you need to stop reading any further while you memorize the above paragraph. Or, copy it down and insert it in your bible. I am teaching you this by the leading and authority from God. I am teaching you something I, myself, have learned by faith. I did not learn this by sitting on a comfortable chair in a carpeted classroom at a university and taking notes from someone lecturing. I have learned this by being at the front lines. I have seen many a promising minister fall because of failure to abide by the above warning.

Let's say you preached an amazing sermon you spent all night preparing, and as a result a multitude of souls rush the altar weeping, repenting and are saved. Hear what I am saying: Humbly give God one hundred percent of the glory. Do not take even one iota of glory for yourself. You might say, "I'm the one who stayed up all night and did the research for that sermon." If you stayed up all night, it's because God gave you the strength. If you did the research and found the answers, it's God that guided you and gave you wisdom to put it together. If multitudes got saved, it's because God prepared their hearts. If they rushed to the altar, it's because God drew them there. Get it?

God is the potter, and you are the pot. Do you brag because, as a pot, you can hold water? Give glory to the Potter! You cannot take even one tenth of one percent of the credit for the anointing on your ministry.

God gets one hundred percent of the glory. Capish?

Part 2

The Anointing Jesus Had While On Earth

Let us now speak of the anointing mentioned in Isaiah 61. This is the anointing that pertains to you. This is the one you need, no matter who you are, in order to effectively and powerfully minister to "the least of these." This is the anointing that you may also call "The Revival" anointing. This anointing will make you a bright spark in the street which will light a great fire. This is the anointing which will bring in results for God in your neighborhood, your city, and eventually will spread in your country and the world.

This is the anointing that you will get if you ask God for it. Jesus had this anointing and He wants YOU to have it! God is looking back and forth on the whole earth searching to whom He can give this anointing.

At this point, we will pause for a brief moment so that you may joyfully raise your hands and say, "Me, Lord, use me, Jesus. I want this anointing!" This anointing is a tough one, but carrying your daily cross is made lighter by the joy that is set before you.

"Let us fix our eyes on Jesus, the author and perfecter of our faith, who for the joy set before him endured the cross, scorning its shame, and sat down at the right hand of the throne of God. Consider him who endured such opposition from sinful men, so that you will not grow weary and lose heart." (Hebrews 12:2, 3)

Also:

"If anyone would come after me, he must deny himself and take up his cross daily and follow me." (Luke 9:23)

"...anyone who does not take his cross and follow me is not worthy of me." (Matthew 10:38)

Right here is where I lose a lot of people. We don't mind hearing about Jesus and the cross, but YOU and the cross? If you have managed to read this far in this book, it may be because God is drawing you closer to himself. With this anointing, the promises of the Scriptures will come to life in and through you in a more fulfilling way than you could have ever imagined. Prepare to position yourself for God's perfect timing of coming events in your life.

Jesus quoted Isaiah 61 at the synagogue at Nazareth. When you read that chapter in Isaiah, you read what Jesus himself has read almost two thousand years ago. You and Jesus have read the very same material. Now, this must be important reading since Jesus made mention of it in His time. He knew they would try to kill him when He mentioned that this scripture would apply to Him and to the Gentiles; and yet, He still read it!

Jews and Gentiles did not mix. The Jews believed God was only for the Jews! Though this was the town He was raised in and He surely knew all of them, they still tried to kill him for saying that the Good News would go to the gentiles.

Isaiah 61 applied to Isaiah; it applied to Jesus, and it applies to you.

"The Spirit of the Sovereign Lord is on me, because the Lord has anointed me to preach good news to the poor." (Isaiah 61:1)

A scripture may be applied in a variety of ways. For example, this scripture is written by Isaiah so it is logical to assume that the Spirit of God was on him, and he was anointed by the Lord to preach the good news to the poor. This may very well be what Isaiah was doing in his time, plus all the other things listed in this chapter.

A scripture or a word of prophecy may be applied to the present and/or the near future and/or the far future. It could apply to you or also to another person or tribe or king or country, or all of the above in different times in history. However, we know that this scripture is a Messianic prophecy because Jesus claimed it for himself. He read verses one and two to the people in His hometown synagogue and then said in **Luke 4:21;**

"Today this scripture is fulfilled in your hearing."

Jesus had the Spirit of the Sovereign Lord ON Him while we have the same spirit now IN us, as Jesus is now IN us. Jesus is ever present IN us.

"I (Jesus) have made you known to them, and will continue to make you known in order that the love you have for me may be in them and that I myself may be in them." (John 17:26)

"...the kingdom of God is within you." (Luke 17:21)

All that Jesus is, all that He has, we have because we have Him IN us. Of course, we did not create the universe as Jesus did, but we are created in His image. We are obviously not the first born of the Spirit as Jesus is, though we also are sons and daughters of God. We were not the perfect sacrifice on the cross to make atonement for all humanity. Jesus was, of course. However, we also "sacrifice ourselves on the cross daily," putting the world behind us so we may serve Him in the perfect way which He has planned for us. Jesus is perfect while we are BEING perfected until that day when we reach our eternity and put on perfection. However, the Holy Spirit, who is perfect, is Jesus IN us.

Part 3

We Can Have The Anointing Jesus Had

At this point, we could start arguing when Jesus received the "anointing." Was it when he was baptized, as he came out of the water? Was it when He returned from His initial forty days of fasting in the desert?

When he left to go in the desert...

"Jesus, full of the Holy Spirit, returned from the Jordan and was led by the Spirit in the desert..." (Luke 4:1)

But when he was done being tempted by the devil in the wilderness...

"Jesus returned to Galilee in the power of the Spirit..." (Luke 4:14)

"Jesus of Nazareth was a man accredited by God to you by miracles, wonders and signs, which God did among you through him." (Acts 2:22)

I do not claim to be a Bible scholar. However, by observation and studies which I have made over the period of my life, I have come to some conclusions. I have seen a pattern on how the Lord works in people. Yes, the Holy Spirit will lead you, and the anointing is not something you "earn." However, I have seen that if you are trustworthy with the little things God gives you to do, sooner or later He will trust you with "The Anointing."

"Because you have been trustworthy in a very small matter, take charge of ten cities." (Luke 19:17)

"...to everyone who has (does the little things), **more will be given, but as for the one who has nothing** (won't do the little things), **even what he has will be taken away." (Luke 19:26)**

As Jesus was tested by the devil, so will you be. As he was tempted in the wilderness, I guarantee you will walk through your own wilderness before you get your anointing. You will wonder, "What is happening to me?" And, "Where are you, Lord, when I need you so much?" And during those times, God will give you something small to do in service to Him.

When you are just about completely financially broke, God will ask you to give your last fifty dollars to someone in need. Don't balk, glorify God. When you and your family seem the least able, the Lord will tell you to invite the poor to eat dinner with you. Feed them and glorify God. When there is something you desperately want to do, but God says, "Do this instead." Just do it and glorify the Holy Name of Jesus. When the Lord tells you to forgive, do it no matter how much you were hurt, so you can be forgiven yourself.

If you are trustworthy with the least, He will give you the most. When you are walking consistently with your eyes on Jesus, you are very close to receiving your anointing.

As in Isaiah 61, we have established that YOU have the Spirit of the Sovereign Lord. So because Jesus is IN you, you have WITHIN you the anointing that comes with faith in Jesus. That anointing is waiting to be manifested in your life if you are found to be trustworthy with the least (or the "least of these"). Jesus tells you that He wants you to have His anointing when, praying to the Holy Father, He says in **John 17:18;**

"As you sent me into the world, I have sent them into the world."

You will be sent in the same manner - with the "anointing."

Part 4

Why The Anointing?

Please pay close attention to the next word I am going to give you because it is so small it is easy to miss; "*to.*" Did you miss it?

"...because the Lord has anointed me *to...*" (Isaiah 61:1)

The anointing is only given in order...to...serve God in a way that will glorify the Holy Name of Jesus, the Sovereign Lord. Whether you are feeding, preaching, teaching, healing, leading, loving (etc.) God's people, you will have God's anointing in order to do it with power. You may be the hammer, but Jesus is the carpenter. Jesus is building, using you. You are used of the Lord in a way that you alone, of course, could not be. Jesus is the power behind you as you are willingly used of Him. You have picked up your daily cross.

I have heard preachers, pastors and evangelists cry out during the emotional moment of a service, "Send your anointing, Lord." They raise their hands above the congregation and cry out, "Give them your anointing, Lord. Heal the sick, Lord and bring miracles to us," as if they controlled God. Some hit the floor and lay there. Some cry out or speak in tongues. And everyone gets happy, and they have a great time in the service. Everyone goes home after the service... and it's life as usual. They may go out to eat lunch or head for the lake or whatever else one may do after a Sunday service.

The problem is that the word "to" has been left out. In other words, the anointing is wanted in order for men to use God. There is no service to God intended. The anointing is wanted in order to have a great time, to spend it upon themselves! I have looked and have found no such anointing listed anywhere in my Bible. Though they pray, there are no genuine miracles of healing in that kind of service.

"When you ask, you do not receive, because you ask with wrong motives, that you may spend what you get on your pleasures." (James 4:3)

When the saints receive an anointing from God, it is to serve God, not for God to serve them. When you receive the "anointing," you will not be the same and life will surely not go on as usual. You will have been changed and going out to lunch will be the last thing on your mind after first receiving the anointing. From that time on, your life will be different. Whereas you were a gifted servant of God, now you are an anointed servant of the Most High God and miracles, signs and wonders may be your way of life as you follow the path God has laid out for you. You have died to the world and are now alive in Christ. Carry your cross.

Part 5

The Revival Anointing

"The Spirit of the Sovereign Lord is on me,

because the Lord has anointed me to preach good news to the poor.

He has sent me to bind up the brokenhearted,

to proclaim freedom for the captives

and release from darkness for the prisoners,

to proclaim the year of the Lord's favor

and the day of vengeance of our God,

to comfort all who mourn, and provide for those who grieve in Zion-

to bestow on them a crown of beauty instead of ashes,

the oil of gladness instead of mourning,

and a garment of praise instead of a spirit of despair."
(Isaiah 61:1-3)

There is a difference between "gifted" and "anointed." A gifted accountant is good at what he does. An anointed accountant miraculously always saves or makes you money. And he gets you excited about God while doing it! That's the kind of accountant I want.

A gifted singer sounds good when you listen to her. However, an anointed singer will move the people to praise God in a greater way. She will lead you to such worship of God so as to bring you to the very threshold of the Holiest and into the very presence of Jesus! And she will give God all the glory.

A gifted preacher will keep your attention. An anointed preacher will present the Word of God in such a way as to captivate your very soul and take you to the next level with God. And miracles may spontaneously occur while he is preaching.

The anointing that Jesus claimed from Isaiah 61 is that spark that set the whole world on fire. It's the revival anointing. There is no reason but for us to continue in that same anointing which Jesus wants us to have. As the first born of the spirit, he is our example. As children of God, we are to follow in His footsteps.

Paul (Saul of Tarsus) was Mr. Religious Intellectual himself. He was gifted with superior intelligence, with amazing zeal and with an ability to communicate exceedingly well. But, he was killing Christians! Then, on the road to Damascus, he had an encounter with Jesus. Then came the anointing. This is what we read about Paul after the anointing:

"My message and my preaching were not with wise and persuasive words, but with a demonstration of the Spirit's power." (1 Corinthians 2:4)

"For the kingdom of God is not a matter of talk but of power." (1 Corinthians 4:20)

As a saved, born again, baptized, Christian living with the indwelling of the Holy Spirit, are you laying hands on the sick and are you now seeing miraculous results daily? As one who is baptized in the Holy Spirit, are you a demonstration of the power of God, with signs and wonders as a way of life? Why not?

No matter what your God-given gifts, you will be used by God to be "a demonstration of the Spirit's power" to glorify the Name of Jesus Christ when you receive the anointing. You will talk less and show God's power more. Less of you, more of Him.

So what did Jesus claim to be anointed to do when he took Isaiah 61 to define His anointing and His life, because His anointing is also your anointing?

1. "...the Lord has anointed me to preach good news to the poor." (v. 1)

Here, the poor means the humble, the oppressed; not only those lacking finances. I strongly suspect that the next few verses of Isaiah 61 will also perfectly describe the "least of these!" You mean to tell me Jesus' amazing spark that lit the greatest revival fire on Earth was a spark in the street? The greatest ministry in the history of the world was a ministry to the "least of these?" **"For you know the grace of our Lord Jesus Christ, that though he was rich, yet for your sakes he became poor, so that you through his poverty might become rich." (2 Corinthians 8:9)**

2. "He has sent me to bind up the brokenhearted..."

Jesus' ministry did not become great because Jesus was sent to the powerful, the wealthy, and the well-known (though they were not left out). His caring, humble ministry was partly built on binding up the brokenhearted. Bind up, here, means to "bandage." Jesus Christ, the Son of God, bandaged your broken heart. He held you up and loved you when your heart was so broken and crushed as to render you helpless. You see, there is no earthly bandage, nor medicine, nor anything else that can heal a broken heart. Only Jesus can do that. It is said "time heals." But as the sufferer of many a broken heart, I'm glad Jesus' anointing took him to the "least of these." God does care for those suffering with the unrelenting pain of a broken heart:

"The Lord is close to the brokenhearted and saves those who are crushed in spirit." (Psalm 34:18)

3. "...to proclaim freedom for the captives." (v. 1)

Here, captives means slaves. Who can deliver those who have been enslaved by Satan through drugs, pornography, greed, alcohol, prostitution, crime, bad temper, etc.? How many are also enslaved by disease? How many are captive to earthly wealth? Jesus has considered you worthy to purchase you with a price – His blood on the cross – and He has delivered you from death. Jesus' anointing took Him to the street to find you, to heal you, and to set you free from your captivity!

"I will keep you and will make you...say to the captives, 'Come out;' and to those in darkness, 'Be free!'" (Isaiah 49:8, 9)

4. "...and release from darkness for the prisoners..." (v. 1)

If you are in the deepest dungeon, the Gospel of Jesus Christ has the power to "free" you. Even though we are all guilty, He forgives us ALL our sins. Jesus' anointing takes Him to the deepest, darkest dungeon man can dig on the face of this Earth to break your chains and release your shackles. Your freedom will also be an eternal freedom when you set foot on the streets of gold where you will be free from the bondage of sin for eternity.

5. "...to proclaim the year of the Lord's favor..." (v. 2)

Thousands of books have been written about the year of the Lord's favor. Suffice it to say that this is the age we are living in now – the age of "grace." God has given us favor - grace. But Jesus had to first die a horrendous death on a bloody cross.

"For it is by grace you have been saved, through faith – and this not from yourselves, it is the gift of God – not by works, so that no one can boast." (Ephesians 2:8, 9)

That special anointing in which Jesus rejoiced took Him to the cross so you could be saved. Jesus saw you as worthy to die for. Salvation is a free gift...to you. Jesus' anointing made Him the Gift of God, the perfect sacrifice. Now, you carry your cross so others may be a recipient of the miracle working grace of Jesus Christ through you.

"See that you also excel in this grace of giving." (2 Corinthians 8:7)

6. "...and the day of vengeance of our God..." (v. 2)

When Jesus quoted Isaiah in His hometown synagogue, he stopped His quotation on the previous line. That may be because this line pertains to a time of judgment in the future when Jesus comes back on earth to judge and subdue all kingdoms and put the earth under His dominion. We too, will be there with Him. Thank you, Jesus!

This anointing will make you truly realize that vengeance is the Lord's, not yours. This will give you a different outlook towards your enemies and those who come against you. You will have a new-found love and forgiveness for them. For as long as a man is alive, there is hope for him to be saved. That's why Stephen, full of grace, could cry out while being stoned to death...

"Lord, do not hold this sin against them." (Acts 7:60)

7. "...to comfort all who mourn, and provide for those who grieve in Zion..." (v. 2, 3)

The word mourn here means "afflicted, saddened." You can help those who mourn only if you have been there yourself (and who hasn't?). Jesus was a man well acquainted with sorrows. Jesus' anointing took Him to the street where He could comfort and love His people and show grace, mercy and pity on the afflicted ones and those who grieved because of their loss. This anointing will also take you to the streets where such abounding love is needed.

"For the Lord comforts his people and will have compassion on his afflicted ones." (Isaiah 49:13)

8. "...to bestow on them a crown of beauty instead of ashes, the oil of gladness instead of mourning, and a garment of praise instead of a spirit of despair." (v. 3)

With this anointing, you will realize that Jesus comes first in your life. The broken hearts, the darkness, the mourning and grieving, the spirit of despair, all the pains that this carnal body suffers are only trials which will make you stronger by the power of the Holy Spirit, your Comforter. Your eyes will be on Jesus, as you lead others with a steady hand of love on the path you are joyfully walking; towards everlasting life with your Father in heaven. There is power in praising the Lord no matter what your circumstances.

9. "They will be called oaks of righteousness, a planting of the Lord..." (v. 3)

Here, "oaks" means "pillars" of justice (righteousness). With this anointing, others will see you as a strong pillar (support) to uphold that which is right in the Lord. In the face of adversity, you will be solidly planted by the Lord to bring that which is right (justice) to the "least of these." In your weakness, you will be made strong; in your poverty, you will be made rich. You will be a beacon of strength to those in need - to the "least of these."

Why do we want this anointing? Why do you want to carry our daily cross? Except Jesus tugs at your heart and the Holy Spirit reveal the Truth to you, you would not know. You pray for and accept this revival anointing in order to personally be a spark in the street to light a great fire of God, to glorify the Lord Jesus Christ and to be used...

10. "...for the display of his splendor." (v. 3)

You are what the angels yearn to look into; you are the joy that was set before Jesus; you are the evidence of God's salvation work; you are the one God so loved that He gave His only Son. You are...

"...the work of my hands, for the display of my splendor. The least of you will become a thousand, the smallest a mighty nation. I am the Lord; in its time I will do this swiftly (will hasten it)**." (Isaiah 60:21, 22)**

CHAPTER *eighteen*

Bright, Neon-Green, Jogging Tights

It would have been simple. It should have been just another beautiful day for some recreation. There is nothing wrong with a little recreation, now and then. But this is how the Lord works, you see. Let me explain...

Sunday afternoons in Northwest Florida in the spring just don't get any better than this...warm, dry, sunny, with a pleasant, gentle breeze. I was driving down the highway which borders the Gulf of Mexico with its clear, tempting, emerald waters. The highway expanded from two to four lanes which in the summer would be bumper to bumper with wide-eyed tourists. However, this was spring and traffic was light. I thought the day was mine to enjoy and be refreshed.

A well-meaning friend had told me about a five-mile, pine tree covered trail just north of the sand dunes. "It ran along the bay," Laura had said, "and there were some oak trees there, also." She had mentioned the alligators, "Be careful of the alligators!" We are used to the alligators down here – not to worry. Laura had said this easy trail was also nicely paved if I wanted to bring my bike. However, "easy" sounded good for today. I'll walk.

I like being at the beach any time of the year because it's always populated with happy vacationers. There are vacationers at all times of the year here because of the mild weather. Even if it's in the fifties in the Winter time, the tourists visiting from Minnesota think it's relatively warm and joyfully find themselves knee deep in the water. Not me! If it's below eighty degrees, it's cold. Still, I find the atmosphere at the beach pleasant and positive. Though I live just twenty minutes from the beach, coming here is like an instant, mini vacation which refreshes me and sets me on a positive track for the coming week.

I, being alone in my car, blessed the Lord out loud when I crossed from Florida into Alabama where I saw that the price of a gallon of gas was forty cents cheaper than in Florida. I rejoiced that my tank was almost empty and I would be able to fill it with cheaper gas before going home. Praise the Lord! I was also looking at restaurants scattered along the roadside to decide where I would eat on the way home from my walk. What a beautiful day. Though I couldn't remember what this morning's sermon was about, I thanked the Lord out loud, "Thank you Jesus. You take such good care of me, Lord!"

Then I saw her on the opposite side of the road, to my left, in her bright, neon-green jogging tights.

Standing next to his cruiser with flashing blue lights, a police officer in the center of the road raised his hand for me to stop. He looked like he had just gotten there. At that point, my comfortable cruising down the highway stopped in a flash moment. He stopped me just even with the lady in bright, neon-green jogging tights. Everything I was looking at then turned to slow motion. I looked to my left, out the driver's side window and could not help but stare at her. Nobody wears bright jogging tights like hers unless they were avid, if not professional, runners. She appeared to be a good-looking lady in her mid-thirties. There was an older couple looking at her and sadly shaking their head.

All along this road were only large, 20-story hotels and condos by the Gulf. She must have been on vacation looking to be refreshed, also. Was she married? Did she have children? What were her plans? Was she having a great time? She probably thought her bright, neon-green jogging tights would make her very visible and keep her safe. Who jogs while on vacation, anyhow? She should have been spending time with her husband, or kids. She should...well...it didn't matter anymore.

She lay face down in a pool of blood on the warm pavement of the entrance to a large hotel by the beach. Her bright, neon-green jogging tights, which she must have dearly loved, blended in perfectly with the tropical landscaping which richly and thickly bordered each side of the driveway to the large hotel. The driver quickly entering the driveway had not seen her, so camouflaged as she was, before he ran into her. She gently bounced off the hood, spun around and hit her head on the pavement, splitting her skull open. She died instantly. She suffered no pain.

She suddenly found herself in eternity, standing in front of the Lord Jesus Christ...if she was saved. Had she glorified God in her life? Had she served the Lord with all her strength, all her mind, all her heart and all her soul? Had she loved and given plentifully in His name? Had she put God first in her life? What did she bring up to heaven with her? How many of her works on Earth will follow her up to heaven? Had she made room in her life to help "the least of these?" Did the Lord say to her, "Come you good and faithful servant" when He saw her coming up?

If she had not believed in Jesus Christ in her life, it was now too late. Her eternity had just been instantly sealed on that warm roadway. Whether she was in hell or heaven, it was now final. Finished.

It is ironic that the very same bright tights she was wearing for visibility and protection became the reason why she died. She had planned on being highly visible. However, at the precise moment when she needed visibility the most, she became invisible, as she blended in with the bright green tropical landscaping.

My heart went out to this young lady and her family. This shocking event immediately brought my mortality under a powerful magnifying glass. The same questions I had asked about her, I now had to ask about myself.

My day, as I had hoped it would have unfolded, was over. I needed to make changes in my life and I had not known how to do it. Just before stepping into eternity, at the very moment of my leaving this Earth, what would the Lord find me doing?

Your death was not in vain, young lady. You went to "sleep," and I awoke.

Whether suddenly, or like a lingering note, this moment of stepping into eternity will come to all of us no matter what we do to evade it or how well we camouflage ourselves so death hopefully doesn't see us. We will then find that our life back on Earth was but a momentary vapor of steam - a very, very thin slice of the time pie. Compared to eternity, **"What is your life? You are a mist that appears for a little while and then vanishes." (James 4:14)** So why do we put so much importance on trivial matters that upset us so much? We instead should be a vessel for loving and giving to others by trusting in our Lord Jesus. We don't truly grasp the meaning of "eternity," nor can we. That is why we must keep our eyes on Jesus and make a foundational decision - what are we living for as we travel this land?

What we must grasp is that when it is dark, we must hold high for the world to see the wonderful saving Light which is Jesus Christ. When we run out of answers for a hurting world, we must put to work in our lives His supernatural, amazing, divine plan which is far greater than anything humanity can conjure up. If you want to be blessed beyond what you deem possible, then dare to go beyond home or church walls, and venture out into the "street." There, you will find the "least of these" waiting to be blessed by the smallest thing you can do for them. Do it in the Name of Jesus while you are still able, as you pass through this thin slice of time; and have something to present to the Lord of Lords as you appear before His glorious presence.

You may be one who is very active. You climb mountains, you travel, you have adventures; you do things others would not dare to do. As exhilarating as these things may be, you will not be able to take them to heaven with you. Will you dare to go beyond the church walls and push beyond human limits, and step into what the Holy Spirit can do in and through you? I guarantee you that serving the Lord in the fullness of His grace, mercy, love and power will be a hundred times more exhilarating than any adventure you can plan or any feeling you can manufacture on this Earth. However, you WILL take to heaven and receive an eternal reward for the works you allow the Holy Spirit to work through you.

My prayer for you is that you may, even for just a moment, behold the splendor of the glory of our Heavenly Father, as you feed and clothe the "least of these." I pray that you may experience the filling of your heart, soul and mind with the excellence of His healing love when, by your obedience to the Holy Spirit, you give a cup of water to the thirsty in the name of Jesus. I pray that His Word is so chiseled on the inside wall of your heart that the lost hear your testimony of Jesus Christ and believe on His Holy Name, and are saved. I pray that you may not just climb the mountain, but toss it into the sea! I pray that you do not just travel across stormy oceans, but calm the angry seas. I pray that whatever little you may have to eat, the Holy Spirit in you may supernaturally multiply it by 5,000 so starving children in the street may eat. I pray for you the humanly impossible which is only possible in the name of Jesus Christ. I pray that when your time comes to go up to be with the Lord, you are fully clothed with the Holy Spirit, and you are right in the midst of doing at least one of the above.

Glory and honor to our Father in heaven, His Son Jesus Christ, and the Holy Spirit.

To all of you who are called to be saints of God, grace and peace be yours in abundance.

APPENDIX A

One Homeless Child of God, One Story

As told by Mari and written by Jean-Luc

I hadn't eaten for three days. The natural urge for another meal was gone. I thought I would never eat again. I had the feeling the Lord wasn't looking out for me. I thought He didn't care. My husband's unexpected death knocked me down, and my DUI finished me off. The street became my new home; the park my bedroom. I felt so lost and alone. I couldn't even cry.

When the Cadillac Escalade pulled up to this lonely heap crumpled on a bench, I thought they were drug dealers, like vultures swooping down. Two fine, middle-aged, black ladies stepped out; all made up and looking very classy. Three sure steps and they were in front of me; then sweetly offered, "Honey, are you hungry?" It made me cry.

The sandwich they put in my hand was the best I ever had. The compassion they showed brought me back to life. They dished out no judgment or preaching, but instead, love and mercy. I felt privileged that someone cared, someone sent by the Lord. They then prayed over me, "Lord, watch over her." Within ten minutes they were gone as fast as they came. But before they left, they left me with this; Jesus my Lord was still in love with me. It made me cry.

That one blessed meal made me want another. It made me want to go on and take care of myself. I don't want to be invisible, as homeless people so often are. I want to be part of society, as over half of the homeless still do. I'm glad two strangers cared for one who was lost...I could have died, and no one would have known. It makes me cry.

Nine of us wait for them expectantly, every time they come so consistently. During rain or shine, just like postal clerks, they load us down with sandwiches and things. But most of all they still tell us about our Lord and Savior whose great joy we are. I'm glad that He has not forgotten me. Now I tell everyone Jesus loves them, and He will never leave nor forsake them. I rejoice that I'm now His disciple, serving my Lord until the day He comes. I now openly share the glorious hope that was so lovingly given to me. That makes me cry with joy.

Knowing that someone like you cares is a good reason for me to keep trying and not give up.

Thank you and God bless you,
Mari

APPENDIX B

Guitarist and Song Writer

This was written by "Tennessee" who is homeless and makes his home under the bridge. He played the guitar in Nashville for a while; and his song writing, singing and guitar playing proves it. He once told me, "I thought I was in bad shape when I didn't have any shoes, until I saw a man that didn't have any feet!"

"Tennessee" testifies that he loves his Lord and Savior, Jesus Christ, without whom he could not survive from day to day.

Love Is A Rose

I say love is like a rose
It only grows on the vine
So you never want to pick your rose
You never want to say it's mine
Just take that beautiful flower
Just don't hold it too tight
'Cause love is a fragile emotion
It has to be handled just right
So make sure the last thing you do at night
And the first thing you do at the break of day
Is thank the Lord for sharing with you
His love for another day

APPENDIX C

Country Boy Loves to Ride

John is homeless and lives in the woods by the railroad tracks. He has the neatest, most well organized camp I have ever seen. He has a spacious "kitchen" where he loves to cook! He was married 32 years, until his wife passed away. That was 18 years ago.

He wears a beautiful cross on a beaded chain around his neck; and he testifies of his love for Jesus Christ, his Lord and Provider. He works when he can. He is a veteran. He has cancer.

I was sitting at his camp with him, one day, and he shared with me this story. He was living way out in the country near Colton, Oregon, at the time.

"I just had to leave the house. My wife was fixing liver and onions, the smell of which makes me sick to my stomach. I took the riding lawnmower and went six miles down the road to the local pub – The White Horse Saloon."

"On my way back, the cops came up behind me and stopped me. They cited me for DUI – being intoxicated while riding my lawnmower! That ticket cost me $180.00!"

"Another time later, I decided to go back to the White Horse Saloon. That time, I rode my horse. I was on my way back home at about ten at night, riding my horse on the shoulder of the road, when the same cop pulls me over, again! He got me for DUI on my horse! He made my wife come get the horse; and he took me to jail, where I spent the night."

Made in the USA
Lexington, KY
26 March 2015